BEADING DESIGN

with semi-precious stones

BEADING DESIGN

with semi-precious stones

KIM GOVER

David and Charles

A DAVID & CHARLES BOOK

David & Charles is an imprint
of F&W Media International, Ltd
Brunel House, Forde Close,
Newton Abbot, TQ12 4PU, UK

F&W Media International, Ltd
is a subsidiary of F+W Media, Inc
10151 Carver Road, Suite #200,
Blue Ash, OH 45242, USA

First published in 2009 in the UK by David & Charles

Reprinted 2011, 2012

Copyright © 2009 Quarto Publishing plc

A catalogue record for this book is available from the British Library.

ISBN-13: 978-0-7153-3011-1

F+W Media Inc. publishes high quality books on a wide range of subjects.
For more great book ideas visit: www.rucraft.co.uk

QUAR.STJ

Conceived, designed and produced by
Quarto Publishing plc
The Old Brewery
6 Blundell Street
London N7 9BH

Project editor: Letitia Luff
Copy editor: Claire Waite Brown
Art director: Caroline Guest
Art editor: Emma Clayton
Designer: Eizabeth Healey
Illustrator: Kuo Kang Chen
Photographer: Martin Norris
Picture research: Sarah Bell

Creative director Moira Clinch
Publisher Paul Carslake

Colour separation by PICA Digital Pte Ltd, Singapore
Printed in China by Toppan Leefung Printers Limited

9 8 7 6 5 4 3

Contents

INTRODUCTION

I first got into jewellery making because I loved buying charms and decided that I could probably make them myself. I did a little research on the Internet, bought some tools and a few basic supplies – and the rest, as they say, is history!

Shopping for materials, especially semi-precious stones and silver, is one of my favourite pastimes. Taking a selection of raw components and shaping them into a statement piece of jewellery gives me a real sense of achievement and pride. I really love the fact that jewellery making can be either a solitary or social pastime, whatever suits your mood. The wonderful online group I belong to provides a lot of inspiration, and I would recommend that everyone joins a group for both the wealth of experience and advice that other members can offer.

Writing this book has been great fun, daunting, and challenging at times but also really interesting. It's been great seeing everything come together in the final stages. The extensive reference section is a handy tool for information about a particular stone, what to coordinate it with, and its metaphysical properties, while the directory itself has fantastic photos and detailed illustrations that will enable you to easily re-create the pieces showcased in this book.

There's a huge diversity of jewellery styles within these pages that I think will be inspirational for experienced artisans and new jewellery makers alike.

K Gaver.

ABOUT THIS BOOK

At the heart of this book is the directory of jewellery, which showcases designs using semi-precious stones and how to re-create them. The directory is preceded by an introduction to the stones and, at the back of the book, you will find information on beading techniques.

THE DIRECTORY (pages 42–111)
This section shows you how to make beautiful pieces of jewellery using semi-precious stones.

The photograph of the finished piece will give you an idea of how your item will look.

The "bead store" lists quantities of semi-precious stones, by size where appropriate, together with other materials you will need to make the piece.

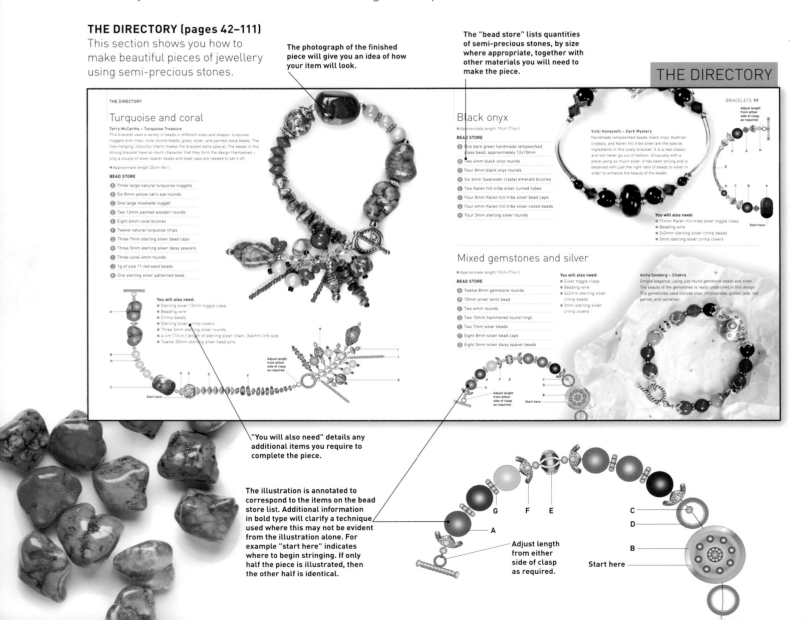

"You will also need" details any additional items you require to complete the piece.

The illustration is annotated to correspond to the items on the bead store list. Additional information in bold type will clarify a technique used where this may not be evident from the illustration alone. For example "start here" indicates where to begin stringing. If only half the piece is illustrated, then the other half is identical.

THE STONES

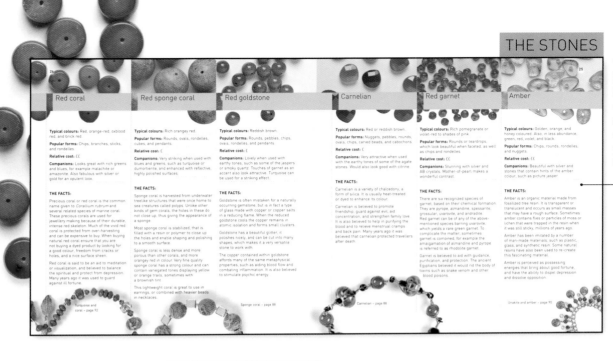

24

Red coral
Typical colours: Red, orange-red, oxblood red, and brick red.
Popular forms: Chips, branches, sticks, and rondelles.
Relative cost: ££
Companions: Looks great with rich greens and blues, for example malachite or amazonite. Also fabulous with silver or gold for an opulent look.

THE FACTS:
Precious coral or red coral is the common name given to *Corallium rubrum* and several related species of marine coral. These precious corals are used for jewellery making because of their durable, intense red skeleton. Much of the vivid red coral is protected from over-harvesting and can be expensive to buy. When buying natural red coral ensure that you are not buying a dyed product by looking for a good colour, freedom from cracks or holes, and a nice surface sheen.

Red coral is said to be an aid to meditation or visualization, and believed to balance the spiritual and protect from depression. Many years ago it was used to guard against ill fortune.

Turquoise and coral – page 92

Red sponge coral
Typical colours: Rich orangey red.
Popular forms: Rounds, ovals, rondelles, cubes, and rondelles.
Relative cost: £
Companions: Very striking when used with blues and greens, such as turquoise or dumortierite, and enhanced with reflective, highly polished surfaces.

THE FACTS:
Sponge coral is harvested from underwater treelike structures that were once home to sea creatures called polyps. Unlike other kinds of gem corals, the holes in these do not close up, thus giving the appearance of a sponge.

Most sponge coral is stabilized, that is, filled with a resin or polymer to close up the holes and enable shaping and polishing to a smooth surface.

Sponge coral is less dense and more porous than other corals, and more orangey red in colour. Very fine quality sponge coral has a strong colour and can contain variegated tones displaying yellow or orange trails, sometimes with a brownish tint.

This lightweight coral is great to use in earrings, or combined with heavier beads in necklaces.

Sponge coral – page 88

Red goldstone
Typical colours: Reddish brown.
Popular forms: Rounds, pebbles, chips, ovals, rondelles, and pendants.
Relative cost: £
Companions: Lovely when used with earthy tones, such as some of the jaspers or smoky quartz. Touches of garnet as an accent also look attractive, highly polished surfaces. Turquoise can be used for a striking effect.

THE FACTS:
Goldstone is often mistaken for a naturally occurring gemstone, but is in fact a type of glass made with copper or copper salts in a reducing flame. When the reduced goldstone cools the copper remains in atomic isolation and forms small clusters.

Goldstone has a beautiful glitter, it polishes nicely, and can be cut into many shapes, which makes it a very versatile stone to work with.

The copper contained within goldstone affords many of the same metaphysical properties, such as aiding blood flow and combating inflammation. It is also believed to stimulate psychic energy.

25

Carnelian
Typical colours: Red or reddish brown.
Popular forms: Nuggets, pebbles, rounds, ovals, chips, carved beads, and cabochons.
Relative cost: £
Companions: Very attractive when used with the earthy tones of some of the agate stones. Would also look good with citrine.

THE FACTS:
Carnelian is a variety of chalcedony, a form of silica. It is usually heat-treated or dyed to enhance its colour.

Carnelian is believed to promote friendship, guard against evil, and concentration, and strengthen family love. It is also believed to help in purifying the blood and to relieve menstrual cramps and back pain. Many years ago it was believed that carnelian protected travellers after death.

Carnelian – page 88

Red garnet
Typical colours: Rich pomegranate or violet-red to shades of pink.
Popular forms: Rounds or teardrops, which look beautiful when faceted, as well as chips and rondelles.
Relative cost: ££
Companions: Stunning with silver and AB crystals. Mother-of-pearl makes a wonderful contrast.

THE FACTS:
There are six recognized species of garnet, based on their chemical formation. They are pyrope, almandine, spessartine, grossular, uvarovite, and andradite. Red garnet can be of any of the above-mentioned species barring uvarovite, which yields a rare green garnet. To complicate the matter, sometimes garnet is comprised, for example the amalgamation of almandine and pyrope is referred to as rhodolite garnet.

Garnet is believed to aid with guidance, purification, and protection. The ancient Egyptians believed it would rid the body of toxins such as snake venom and other blood poisons.

Amber
Typical colours: Golden, orange, and honey coloured. Also, in less abundance, green, red, violet, and black.
Popular forms: Chips, rounds, rondelles, and nuggets.
Relative cost: ££
Companions: Beautiful with silver and stones that contain hints of the amber colour, such as picture jasper.

THE FACTS:
Amber is an organic material made from fossilized tree resin. It is transparent or translucent and occurs as small masses that may have a rough surface. Sometimes amber contains flies or particles of moss or lichen that were trapped in the resin when it was still sticky, millions of years ago.

Amber has been imitated by a number of man-made materials, such as plastic, glass, and synthetic resin. Some natural resins have also been used to re-create this fascinating material.

Amber is perceived as possessing energies that bring about good fortune, and have the ability to dispel depression and dissolve opposition.

Unakite and amber – page 92

**THE STONES
(pages 16–41)**
Photographs of the most common forms of each semi-precious stone, organized by colour, help you identify those you wish to buy and use.

Detailed information about each stone enables you to compare one stone with another and plan how you will use them in your own designs.

CORE TECHNIQUES

**CORE TECHNIQUES
(pages 112–123)**
You may wish to refer to the core techniques section for further beading instructions.

CORE TECHNIQUES

CORE TECHNIQUES 119

Wrapping individual beads
This is an easy way to embellish a plain bead, using wires and a few other beads.

Tools and materials
- Wire: 0.8mm (20-gauge) (3 x the length of bead) and 0.6mm (22-gauge) (12 x the length of bead)
- Wire cutters
- Pliers: round-nosed and flat-nosed

Fit the spiral inside the hole in the bead if possible.

1. Cut a length of 0.8mm (20-gauge) wire. Make a closed loop (see page 115). Now cut a long length of 0.6mm (22-gauge) wire. Use the round-nosed pliers to make a tiny spiral at the end of this length. Slide the spiral over the thicker wire and thread both of them into the bead, from the bottom.

2. Holding everything very firmly in your hand, start to wrap the 0.6mm (22-gauge) wire around the bead. When you have made one wrap, thread some of the small beads onto the wire and continue to wrap, spacing the beads into the wraps as you work.

Hold and wrap as tightly as you can.

3. When you reach the top of the bead, wrap the wire as firmly around the bead as possible, then move the thinner wire back onto the thicker one. Wind around this a few times. Clip off the extra length and flatten in the end.

4. Push this spiral as close into the bead as you can, then add another bead to the 0.8mm (20-gauge) wire and make a closed loop above it. Trim the wire and flatten in the end.

Wire on wire wrapping
Wrapping with two different wires will create other decorative results. Start in the same way but attach a third, longer length of finer wire to the wrapping wire. Wrap this around the main wrapping wire as you wind up the main bead. Finish off in the same way as shown here.

5. To tighten the wire around the beads, use the tips of flat-nosed pliers against the wire and turn each wrap to make an angle in the wire. Do this as many times as you like, making sure you don't damage the bead or the wire. Be careful not to over-tighten to the extent that the wire snaps.

Coils
These can be used as decorative head pins for drop earrings or incorporated into other designs.

Tools and materials
- Wire
- Wire cutters
- Pliers: round-nosed and flat-nosed

A larger loop in the centre will create a different look.

1. Cut a length of wire and make a loop with the smallest point of the round-nosed pliers.

2. Position the flat-nosed pliers across the loop to hold it firmly, but without marking the wire. Use your fingers to wind the length of wire around the loop to create a coil.

3. The coil can be finished with a simple loop, as shown here, or a closed loop.

Zigzag spacers
Zigzag spacers work well in either earrings or necklaces. This is an excellent design with which to experiment with hammering. Ideally you need a small block to hammer onto, and you need a small hammer, but it is fine to experiment with household tools and smooth surfaces.

Tools and materials
- Wire
- Wire cutters
- Pliers: round-nosed and flat-nosed
- Hammer and block (optional)

1. Cut two lengths of wire and put one aside to be used as a measure. Make a loop at the end around round-nosed pliers.

2. Continue to turn the wire in the same way so it zigzags from side to side. At the end of the zigzag, make a final turn with the pliers, then turn the wire back onto itself. Clip off the excess wire.

3. Hammer the spacer, if desired, to give extra strength. This will slightly increase its size, so you may want to re-scale your design before making more. The spacers can be linked with simple or closed loops.

Step-by-step instructions take you through the key beading techniques needed to re-create the pieces in the directory.

Clear photographs show you how to give your jewellery a professional finish.

Materials and Tools

When working with beads it is possible to achieve very impressive results without needing to invest in a huge range of materials and tools. You can start with a small selection and build up your collection as you develop your skills.

Materials

The thread you select for your chosen project will depend on the size and weight of beads you are using and the technique you intend to use. Beading wires such as Soft Flex or Beadalon are strong multi-strand steel cables coated in nylon; you may come across tiger tail, which is also a beading wire, but usually with a lesser number of strands. The higher the number of multi-strand wires the less they are prone to kinking. Both types of wire are best finished with crimps. My personal preference is 2x2mm sterling silver crimps for strength, finished with 3mm or 4mm crimp covers.

Synthetic threads are usually worked with needles and are available in different thicknesses, while natural threads such as silk and linen are available in various sizes and colours but do not have the strength of the synthetic versions. Some beading threads are already waxed, but if not, you will need to purchase some beeswax or thread conditioner to enable you to work with them more easily.

Metal wire can be obtained in a range of finishes, sizes, and hardnesses. All of the designs in this book that contain wire components have listed the approximate diameter (or gauge) as well as the material and, where appropriate, the hardness. For example: sterling silver, half hard. If you are combining wire with chain, it is best to match the link size to the gauge of your wire.

Silver Beads

When purchasing "silver" beads care should be taken to ensure that you receive exactly what you are expecting. Sterling silver is usually more expensive than Bali or Karen hill tribe silver. Remember components with high pure silver contents are softer and will become dented or marked quickly. Silver-plated, silver tone, or Tibetan beads are a great alternative if you're on a budget.

- **Sterling silver:** An alloy containing 92.5% pure silver and 7.5% other metals (usually copper) often stamped .925.
- **German silver:** This may be marked 800 or 900 (either 80% or 90% pure silver).
- **Bali silver:** Traditional Bali silver normally contains a minimum of 92.5% pure silver.
- **Thai or Karen hill tribe silver:** This is categorized as "fine silver", meaning that the pure silver content is 95% to 99%. There is no hallmarking system in Thailand.
- **Tibetan silver:** Original Tibetan silver may contain a silver content of up to 99.9%, but silver marked as Tibetan can contain anything from 1% or 2% up to 70% pure silver. It may be an alloy containing lead, copper, and often nickel, which can be an irritant. Vendors should be able to advise you of the precise silver content of their beads.
- **Silver-plated or silver tone:** These beads will either be an alloy, silver in colour, or have a very fine coating of sterling silver plating on top, which may wear off over time.

Tools

By obtaining the tools listed below you will be well equipped to undertake the projects shown in this book.

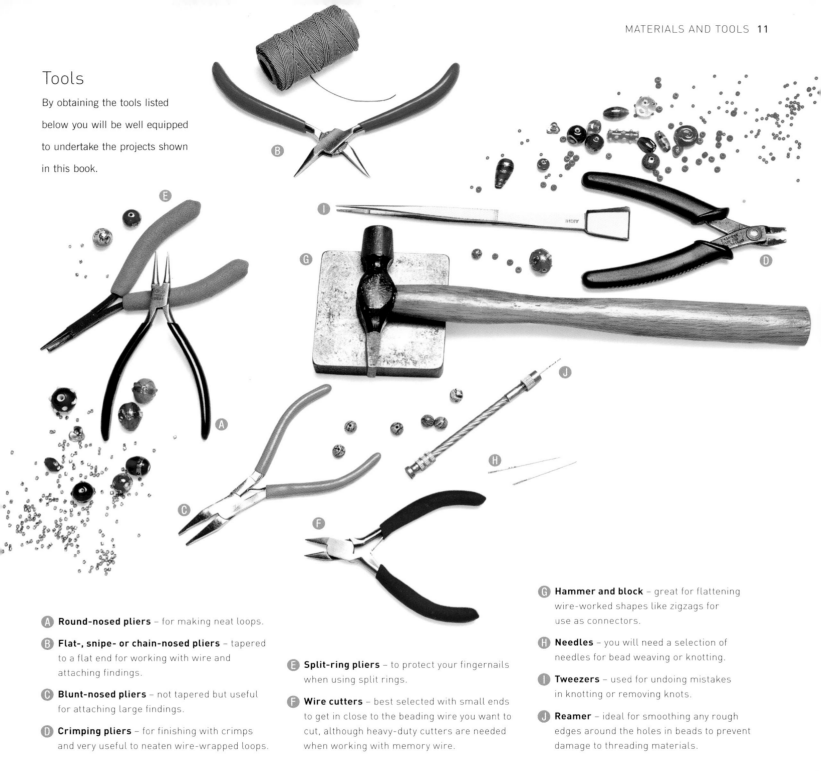

A **Round-nosed pliers** – for making neat loops.

B **Flat-, snipe- or chain-nosed pliers** – tapered to a flat end for working with wire and attaching findings.

C **Blunt-nosed pliers** – not tapered but useful for attaching large findings.

D **Crimping pliers** – for finishing with crimps and very useful to neaten wire-wrapped loops.

E **Split-ring pliers** – to protect your fingernails when using split rings.

F **Wire cutters** – best selected with small ends to get in close to the beading wire you want to cut, although heavy-duty cutters are needed when working with memory wire.

G **Hammer and block** – great for flattening wire-worked shapes like zigzags for use as connectors.

H **Needles** – you will need a selection of needles for bead weaving or knotting.

I **Tweezers** – used for undoing mistakes in knotting or removing knots.

J **Reamer** – ideal for smoothing any rough edges around the holes in beads to prevent damage to threading materials.

Buying Gemstones

Where to buy

Personal recommendation is the best way to select the source of your stones to begin with, but always choose your stones because you like them.

Bead shows

Bead shows are held at various times of the year. They give the buyer an opportunity to compare gemstones from different dealers. The stones are laid out in many strings, with various colours, grades, and sizes ready to be inspected for cut and quality. The dealer will be able to tell you where the stones have come from and what treatments they have received.

When buying semi-precious gemstones there can be many factors to consider before making your purchase. The price you pay will be influenced by the abundance and popularity of the stone, whether it has been treated or not, and to what degree it has been cut, faceted, and polished. Where you buy the stones will also affect the purchase price.

Bead stores

Beads in a bead store are laid out for you to view in person. You can touch them and ask the sales person about them, although the retailer may not have as much specialist knowledge of the stones as a dealer would, depending on where the store sources them from. Stones may be more expensive to purchase due to the store's overhead cost.

Semi-precious gemstones are variable so, if possible, pick them up to have a close look at them before you buy.

Online suppliers

There are some excellent semi-precious gemstone retailers on the Internet, who give full and frank descriptions of their stones, including any treatments used on them. Look for someone who is prepared to offer a full refund if you are not satisfied with your purchase: they will offer this because their commercial success depends on their good reputation. Bear in mind when Internet shopping that the photographs may not necessarily represent the exact stones you will be buying, so read any descriptions carefully.

Online auction sites

You can buy semi-precious beads from one of several online auction sites. Many of the sellers on these sites are well established with excellent service and good-quality gemstones. However, there are also a number of unscrupulous sellers who use the anonymity of this style of trading to sell poor-quality stones or stones that have been dyed to look like more expensive gemstones.

Before trading with any auction-site sellers, you should take a good look at their feedback ratings. Avoid trading with any sellers with poor feedback.

Buying abroad

Once you have used semi-precious gemstones a lot you will begin to feel confident in recognizing them, as well as in spotting stones that are being passed off as other gemstones. When you are confident, buying abroad can be a great way to pick up unusual stones at good prices, or stones that you may not be able to source at home.

Grading

The grading system for precious stones, such as rubies or emeralds, is fairly rigid. The GIA (Gemological Institute of America) system, used internationally, divides the translucent stones into three types and assesses them according to clarity. The grades range from I3, the lowest grade, where the inclusions are very obvious and have a negative overall effect on the stone in question, up to VVS, which means that the specimen has very slight inclusions that are not visible to the naked eye but can be seen through 10x magnification – for example with a jeweller's loupe. The highest grade is IF, which is internally flawless.

You can while away hours choosing between a huge variety of semi-precious gemstones.

However, the grading system for semi-precious, opaque stones is not as clearly defined. You will most commonly encounter stones graded by letter, for example from AAA, which is classed as an extremely good specimen, ranging down to C or D, which are still nice stones to use in jewellery, although they may have visible imperfections. Often stones will not be graded at all, but sold with a description stating their condition, or no description at all. In this instance buying because you like them and checking that the seller has a good returns policy is the way to go.

Gemstone treatments

Coloured semi-precious gemstones are often treated in some way to enhance their appearance. Some treatments, such as heat treatment, have a permanent effect, others, such as some of the dyeing or staining techniques, do not. Gemstones that are not believed to be enhanced through any of these methods include iolite, peridot, malachite, hematite, chrysoberyl, and the entire feldspar group, which includes labradorite, moonstone, amazonite, and sunstone.

Staining and dyeing

Many stones with porous surfaces are dyed or stained to enhance their natural colour. For example, purple crazy agate is simply crazy agate enhanced with a purple dye that picks up the stone's variations in colour, with striking effect. Many pearls are also dyed to achieve countless colours. Check for dyeing by inspecting the drill hole, where you will find a collection of darker dye. On clear gemstones, such as rose quartz, the dye may be visible in the cracks, which will appear darker.

Whether the dyeing of a natural stone is acceptable or not is dependent on whether the stone has been dyed to enhance its natural colouring, or dyed to deceive buyers. For example, howlite is often dyed to mimic lapis lazuli or turquoise, and sold as a natural stone for a higher price. Quite often, stones are dyed to mask the fact that they are of inferior material. A simple test to check for dye in this case is to rub over the stone with acetone nail polish remover on a cotton ball. If it is dyed, then some colour residue will appear on the cotton ball after a while.

Heating

The heating of gemstones is extremely common and can be used to clear internal inclusions and to lighten, darken, or completely change the colour of the stone. Heat treatment can normally only be detected by an expert under laboratory conditions. One of the gemstones commonly treated in this way is amethyst, which may be heated up to turn to citrine. A portion of the stone is then irradiated (see below) to turn it back to amethyst, creating a very attractive, multi-tonal stone. Naturally occurring citrine is quite rare, and if it were not for heat treatments, the cost of citrine would be much higher. Other gemstones routinely heat treated include aquamarine, light green tourmaline, and amazonite.

Irradiation

This treatment involves targeting a gemstone with subatomic particles or radiation. The most common stones treated in this manner are amethyst (see above) and blue topaz, which occurs naturally in quite a pale blue, but when irradiated can achieve a stunningly vivid colour. This treatment is not always permanent, and in some cases exposure of the treated stone to heat and light may cause the colour to fade. In the United States irradiated stones are regulated to ensure there is no harmful residual radiation.

Stabilizing

Stabilizing procedure uses binders, such as certain polymers, that are soaked into the stone to add strength and durability. Stabilizing is a treatment commonly used for turquoise, because this stone is too unstable to use for jewellery in its natural state. The fact that turquoise has been stabilized should not deter anyone from purchasing it. However, buyers should note that stabilized turquoise differs from reconstituted turquoise, where the stone has been completely ground up, had binders added, and then been reformed into new shapes. There is no problem with buying turquoise in this form, as long as it is made clear exactly what is being sold. Reconstituted turquoise, rather than natural stabilized turquoise, is considerably cheaper.

Diffusion

Surface diffusion is normally used where a heat treatment has not been successful in changing the colour of the stone. The treatment involves the

infusion of chemicals into the surface of the stone
at high temperatures. If the surface of the stone
needs polishing at a later date, then the colour
may be affected because it does not run deep.
This process can also be used to create stars
within the stone – however they will only be a few
millimetres deep and may not be permanent.

Oiling, waxing, and fracture filling

For many hundreds of years emeralds have
been oiled or waxed to fill in their cracks and
improve their appearance – a perfect unoiled
emerald would be a rarity and could command a
huge price tag. Alexandrite and rubies have also
occasionally been treated in this manner. Fracture
filling also improves the appearance of surface
fractures by using colourless substances that
match the light refraction of the stone, such as
oils, resins, polymers, or even glass.

Bleaching

This process is used on organic materials such
as pearls, coral, or ivory. The bleaching process
lightens the substance and is a permanent and
undetectable treatment that does not affect the
cost of the piece.

Chapter one
THE STONES

This resource – organized by colour – showcases all the essential semi-precious stones and describes their characteristics. You can look up stones that match a colour theme, or colour-match a prized stone in your collection. There are also tips to avoid buying fake, dyed, or valueless stones.

Jet

Typical colours: Black or dark brown.

Popular forms: Rounds and ovals, often carved, teardrops, bicones, and rondelles.

Relative cost: ££

Companions: Due to its neutral colour, anything could be matched with jet to achieve subtle or dramatic effect.

THE FACTS:

Jet is not a mineral but an organic material composed of carbonized wood.

Easily polished, jet lends itself well to the creation of jewellery. It was popularly used in mourning jewellery in the 1800s and as part of the flapper fashion in the 1920s.

Jet was used long ago to protect against the evil eye and is therefore perceived as a good talisman for protection. Those who use it as a healing stone believe it can banish headaches and stomach pains, and help to control epilepsy.

Jet and coral – page 107

Black onyx

Typical colours: Black.

Popular forms: Rounds, chips, cabochons, faceted nuggets, and pendants.

Relative cost: £

Companions: Due to the neutral colour of the stone, anything could be matched with it for a subtle or dramatic effect. Pearls in particular look fabulous with onyx.

THE FACTS:

Onyx is a form of quartz that ranges from white through almost every colour apart from blue or purple. Black onyx is common and very well known.

Most of the commercially produced onyx is heat-treated and then dyed to enhance its colour.

Onyx is believed to help the wearer overcome grief and to bring fortune.

Blue coral and lava stone – page 60

Blackstone

Typical colours: Black.

Popular forms: Rounds, ovals, teardrops, and carved focals.

Relative cost: £

Companions: Can be used with absolutely anything for a striking effect.

THE FACTS:

Blackstone is often perceived to be a stone in its own right, but in truth may be made from a variety of stones, most commonly jasper, which can easily be permanently enhanced with dye, and polishes nicely.

Blackstone can be used as a cheaper alternative to black onyx, although it doesn't have quite such a shiny finish.

The spiritual properties of this stone will vary according to the natural stone that has been dyed.

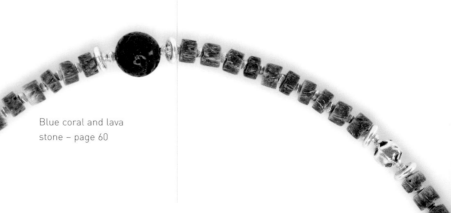

Lava stone

Typical colours: Black, dark brown, or grey.

Popular forms: Rounds, ovals, slices, discs, rondelles, teardrops, and saucers.

Relative cost: £

Companions: This stone is neutral and has quite a matte finish, so would look stunning with silver and highly reflective crystals to add colour.

THE FACTS:

Lava stone is basalt, molten rock, that has been ejected from an erupting volcano. It usually has a fine grain due to cooling rapidly on the surface of the earth. The kind most often used for beads has a vesicular texture, with small cavities produced as gas or steam expanded during the solidification of the rock.

Lava stone is a fascinating, versatile, and exotic material to use in jewellery design, and is wonderfully tactile.

Lava stone is believed to promote physical and mental strength in difficult situations, and was used by the American Indians when going into battle.

Labradorite

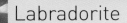

Typical colours: Greyish blue to smoky black with flashes of green, blue-orange, and red.

Popular forms: Rounds, ovals, coins, nuggets, and faceted shapes.

Relative cost: ££

Companions: Abalone shell, silver, moonstone, and crystals.

THE FACTS:

Labradorite is a dull grey feldspar mineral that displays a wonderful play of colour – also known as schiller – when viewed from certain angles. The schiller is created when refracted light travels through different layers of the stone. The colours are intense and range from reds and oranges to blues, greens, and violets.

Labradorite is said to be a stone that can banish fear and insecurity, fire the imagination, and bring clarity of thought. It is also believed to attract success.

Labradorite – page 101

Hematite

Typical colours: Black to steel grey, also found in brown to red forms.

Popular forms: Rounds, ovals, and rice beads, as well as many other shapes, such as stars, hearts, and donuts.

Relative cost: £

Companions: Hematite looks fantastic when contrasted with mother-of-pearl, and is also commonly used as a spacer or accent bead.

THE FACTS:

Hematite is the mineral form of iron. It is harder than pure iron, but care must be taken because it is also brittle.

This extremely popular gemstone was one of the most used stones in the ancient world.

Of its many properties, hematite is believed to reflect negativity back to its source, reduce stress, and act as an aid for good sleep. It is sometimes used for divination as a scrying tool, and is believed to promote mental clarity and intuition.

Moonstone

Typical colours: White, peach, and grey.

Popular forms: Rounds, ovals, chips, bricks, and faceted shapes.

Relative cost: ££

Companions: Garnet, amethyst, pearls, and silver suit designs using moonstone.

THE FACTS:

Moonstone is the opalescent variant of orthoclase, a mineral that forms in igneous rock.

Moonstone takes its name from its shimmering play of pale blue that is reminiscent of the moon. This shimmering is referred to as adularisation and is caused by the internal construction of the gemstone and the way the light is refracted through it.

In some places, moonstones are said to be able to bring about lovely dreams. This stone is also said to improve intuition and increase sensitivity.

Jade – page 97

Quartz

Typical colours: Clear, frosted, green, lemon, and blue.

Popular forms: Many faceted shapes as well as rounds, coins, ovals, and cushions.

Relative cost: £

Companions: The wide range of colours in quartz can easily be matched with any gemstone in your bead store, or used simply with silver or gold.

THE FACTS:

Various kinds of quartz have been used for many years in jewellery and decorative items. Generally quartz is very affordable as a gemstone and appears in a wide variety of colours according to the minerals present and the conditions in which it has been created.

Rutilated quartz has needlelike crystals within it that may be yellow, black, or red and appear slightly metallic. Tourmalinated quartz has needles of black tourmaline inside and is fascinating to look at. Lemon and green quartz are often heated to enhance their colours, and look stunning when faceted.

Clear quartz is believed to enhance the metaphysical properties of other gemstones when they are used together. It is also said to be a useful aid for meditation.

Jade

Typical colours: Green, lilac, white, cream, pink, brown, red, blue, black, orange, and yellow.

Popular forms: Rounds, tubes, ovals, and rondelles.

Relative cost: £

Companions: Beautiful when used with silver and crystals to enhance its many colour variants.

THE FACTS:

There are two types of recognized jade: jadeite and nephrite. Both are tough forms of rock that lend themselves well to carving and polishing.

Jadeite is found in metamorphic rock and appears in a wide range of colours, including green, lilac, white, pink, brown, red, blue, black, orange, and yellow. The most highly prized is imperial jade, which, due to its chromium content, is a very rich emerald green.

Nephrite is found in metamorphic and igneous rocks and is formed from an aggregate of amphibole crystals that form a structure stronger than steel. Its colours vary from dark green, due to rich iron content, to cream colours resulting from magnesium content.

Jade is believed to possess calming properties and have the ability to aid with mental clarity, wisdom, and courage.

White agate

Typical colours: Semi-translucent white with white to yellowish white banding.

Popular forms: Rounds, nuggets, rice beads, tubes, and coins.

Relative cost: £

Companions: Very effective with stones such as garnet and smoky quartz but can add dramatic effect when used with any stone.

THE FACTS:

Agate is a member of the quartz family and there are many colour variations and patterns available. It is very durable, easily worked into many shapes, and polishes nicely, in fact its natural colours can be greatly enhanced through polishing.

White agate is an attractive stone, especially the banded type, which shows lovely soft colour variations, and can be worked wonderfully into many jewellery designs.

Agate stones are believed to have protective and comforting properties, and are often carried as talismans.

Opal

Typical colours: Pale pink, blue, yellow, green, white, or grey.

Popular forms: Nuggets, faceted rectangles, and chips.

Relative cost: ££

Companions: Silver and gold set these stones off nicely. Smoky quartz can be used to pick out some of the markings on the opal stones.

THE FACTS:

Opal is really classed as a precious stone, but there are common or non-precious forms. Potch is the name given to a form of common opal, and a huge percentage of the opal mined is potch. Common opal is mostly opaque and doesn't show a play of colour within it.

The background colour generally ranges from milky white, pale pink, or pale grey to black. These colours are created by impurities in the silica that appeared in the formation of the opal.

Opal may be dendritic, meaning that it has treelike or mosslike patterning through it.

Pink opal is said to enhance mental clarity and to promote spiritual awareness.

Opal and Botswana agate – page 56

Mother-of-pearl

Typical colours: Naturally black or white with touches of brown, but may be dyed to any colour.

Popular forms: Carved focals and pendants.

Relative cost: £

Companions: Especially attractive when used in a monochromatic colour scheme and enhanced with silver or gold.

THE FACTS:

Mother-of-pearl is formed by molluscs. It coats the inner surface of the shell to defend the mollusc against parasites.

Mother-of-pearl is absolutely beautiful when carved with a design such as a flower or a butterfly and used as a focal piece in jewellery. It is iridescent and widely used for decorative purposes in interior design and for buttons on clothes, as well as in jewellery.

Believed to be a protective stone, mother-of-pearl is also thought to enhance intuition and adaptability and help with decision making.

Pearls

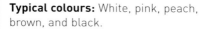

Typical colours: White, pink, peach, brown, and black.

Popular forms: Rounds, baroques, and coins.

Relative cost: ££

Companions: Stunning with abalone, seashells, silver, and sea-coloured stones such as apatite or blue topaz.

THE FACTS:

A pearl is made when a bivalve creature, such as an oyster or clam, builds up a protective layer of nacre around a piece of grit or a foreign body as a defence against that which has found its way into the shell. The nacre builds up in layers and the refraction of light through these layers is what gives the lustre to the pearl. The colour of the pearl is determined by the natural colour of the nacre in the mollusc, but pearls are often dyed many colours.

Natural pearls occur without human intervention, but often many molluscs must be opened before a pearl is found, which makes natural pearls expensive. Cultured pearls are farmed and small beads are introduced to the mollusc to encourage a buildup of the nacre around them.

Tahitian black pearls from the black-lipped oyster are highly prized for their beauty and rarity.

Pearls are believed to represent faith.

Rose quartz

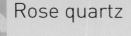

Typical colours: From very pale pink to almost rose red shades.

Popular forms: Rounds, ovals, coins, and carved focals.

Relative cost: £

Companions: Beautiful when matched with silver and rich pink or pale blue crystals.

THE FACTS:

This pretty stone is widely available in colours ranging from palest pink to rich rose and can be cut into many attractive shapes for beads. It belongs to the quartz family, as the name indicates, and its colouring is attributed to trace amounts of titanium, iron, and manganese.

Although not generally cut into fine gemstones, because it is often cloudy, when used in rounds and hearts, for example, rose quartz makes beautifully soft-hued stones that work wonderfully in delicate, feminine jewellery designs.

Rose quartz is believed to aid you in knowing and accepting your inner self.

Pearl – page 110

Pink opal

Typical colours: Pink with dark pink, grey, or sometimes creamy markings throughout.

Popular forms: Nuggets, discs, cylinders, ovals, and rounds.

Relative cost: ££

Companions: Beautiful with other softly toned stones, such as white agate, for a subtle effect, or teamed with something more striking, such as jet, onyx, or labradorite, for a dramatic look.

THE FACTS:

There are two varieties of opal, precious and common. Precious opals have an iridescent play of colour within them. They are expensive and used in fine jewellery. Common opals do not have this play of colour inside but are still wonderful to work with. They often have subtle variations in colour, from greys through to creams.

Opal is a hardened silica gel containing 5 to 20 per cent water. Due to their water content, opals can become brittle and must be taken good care of: they must not be stored where they can be exposed to heat. Opal jewellery should be worn often to enable it to absorb humidity from the air and the wearer's skin.

Pink opal is used as a stone of peace for the aura, and is said to enable the healing of emotions.

Rhodochrosite

Typical colours: Rose-red.

Popular forms: Rounds, teardrops, ovals, and nuggets.

Relative cost: ££

Companions: Complemented by the black of onyx or blackstone for a striking effect, or use white and grey stones, such as mother-of-pearl or Botswana agate, to bring out the variations in the lower-graded stones. Silver and crystals add sparkle and enhance the colours.

THE FACTS:

Rhodochrosite is a manganese carbonate material that is rose-red in its pure form, while impure forms can range from shades of pink to pale brown. Choosing A-graded stones will be expensive but will provide beads of a wonderful light raspberry red. Using lower grade stones can be just as rewarding because they display dark and light pink lacy patterns, often with small streaks of grey running through.

Rhodochrosite is believed to have many positive properties, including drawing love to the wearer, improving eyesight, and helping to relieve stress.

Rhodochrosite – page 103

Pink coral

Typical colours: Rich pink (rare) and pale pink (angel skin variety).

Popular forms: Rounds or small branches.

Relative cost: £££

Companions: Stunning when left to its natural beauty, perhaps enhanced with just a few crystals and silver.

THE FACTS:

Coral used in jewellery is not often found in reefs but in branchlike structures that resemble underwater trees. Coral structures are actually formed when small colonizing marine creatures collect calcium carbonate around their bodies.

The value of pink coral depends on how rare it is. The slower-growing varieties are highly prized but they are endangered and mostly protected from harvesting because they do not replenish quickly. Therefore, if you want some real, natural pink coral beads you may be able to find vintage pieces, but they will be highly priced. An alternative to buying natural pink coral is to buy sea bamboo coral, which is dyed to enhance the colour and is much less expensive. Otherwise buy oxblood coral, which has a natural red colour.

Fire agate

Typical colours: Brown, orange-brown, and deep red.

Popular forms: Rounds, nuggets, teardrops, and coins.

Relative cost: ££

Companions: Earth tones, silver, and crystals in colours that pick out the fire in the bead all work well.

THE FACTS:

This rock is formed in layers. Where the layers are thin light enters into them, resulting in a play of colours referred to as "fire". When cutting fire agate into stones and beads the layers are gradually filed and polished away until only the fire is visible. Care must be taken not to take away too many layers and ruin the stone.

Fire agate is often heat-treated or dyed to enhance its colours and patterns.

Fire agate is perceived as a stone of courage and strength, and one that brings strong grounding powers. It is used in healing for the stomach and the nervous and endocrine systems.

Fire agate – page 55

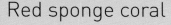

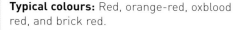

Red coral

Typical colours: Red, orange-red, oxblood red, and brick red.

Popular forms: Chips, branches, sticks, and rondelles.

Relative cost: ££

Companions: Looks great with rich greens and blues, for example malachite or amazonite. Also fabulous with silver or gold for an opulent look.

THE FACTS:

Precious coral or red coral is the common name given to *Corallium rubrum* and several related species of marine coral. These precious corals are used for jewellery making because of their durable, intense red skeleton. Much of the vivid red coral is protected from over-harvesting and can be expensive to buy. When buying natural red coral ensure that you are not buying a dyed product by looking for a good colour, freedom from cracks or holes, and a nice surface sheen.

Red coral is said to be an aid to meditation or visualization, and believed to balance the spiritual and protect from depression. Many years ago it was used to guard against ill fortune.

Turquoise and coral – page 92

Red sponge coral

Typical colours: Rich orangey red.

Popular forms: Rounds, ovals, rondelles, cubes, and pendants.

Relative cost: £

Companions: Very striking when used with blues and greens, such as turquoise or dumortierite, and enhanced with reflective, highly polished surfaces.

THE FACTS:

Sponge coral is harvested from underwater treelike structures that were once home to sea creatures called polyps. Unlike other kinds of gem corals, the holes in these do not close up, thus giving the appearance of a sponge.

Most sponge coral is stabilized, that is filled with a resin or polymer to close up the holes and enable shaping and polishing to a smooth surface.

Sponge coral is less dense and more porous than other corals, and more orangey red in colour. Very fine quality sponge coral has a strong colour and can contain variegated tones displaying yellow or orange trails, sometimes with a brownish tint.

This lightweight coral is great to use in earrings, or combined with heavier beads in necklaces.

Red goldstone

Typical colours: Reddish brown.

Popular forms: Rounds, pebbles, chips, ovals, rondelles, and pendants.

Relative cost: £

Companions: Lovely when used with earthy tones, such as some of the jaspers or smoky quartz. Touches of garnet as an accent also look attractive. Turquoise can be used for a striking effect.

THE FACTS:

Goldstone is often mistaken for a naturally occurring gemstone, but is in fact a type of glass made with copper or copper salts in a reducing flame. When the reduced goldstone cools the copper remains in atomic isolation and forms small clusters.

Goldstone has a beautiful glitter, it polishes nicely, and can be cut into many shapes, which makes it a very versatile stone to work with.

The copper contained within goldstone affords many of the same metaphysical properties, such as aiding blood flow and combating inflammation. It is also believed to stimulate psychic energy.

Sponge coral – page 88

Carnelian

Typical colours: Red or reddish brown.

Popular forms: Nuggets, pebbles, rounds, ovals, chips, carved beads, and cabochons.

Relative cost: £

Companions: Very attractive when used with the earthy tones of some of the agate stones. Would also look good with citrine.

THE FACTS:

Carnelian is a variety of chalcedony, a form of silica. It is usually heat-treated or dyed to enhance its colour.

Carnelian is believed to promote friendship, guard against evil, aid concentration, and strengthen family love. It is also believed to help in purifying the blood and to relieve menstrual cramps and back pain. Many years ago it was believed that carnelian protected travellers after death.

Carnelian – page 88

Red garnet

Typical colours: Rich pomegranate or violet-red to shades of pink.

Popular forms: Rounds or teardrops, which look beautiful when faceted, as well as chips and rondelles.

Relative cost: ££

Companions: Stunning with silver and AB crystals. Mother-of-pearl makes a wonderful contrast.

THE FACTS:

There are six recognized species of garnet, based on their chemical formation. They are pyrope, almandine, spessarite, grossular, uvarovite, and andradite. Red garnet can be of any of the above-mentioned species barring uvarovite, which yields a rare green garnet. To complicate the matter, sometimes garnet is combined, for example the amalgamation of almandine and pyrope is referred to as rhodolite garnet.

Garnet is believed to aid with guidance, purification, and protection. The ancient Egyptians believed it would rid the body of toxins such as snake venom and other blood poisons.

Amber

Typical colours: Golden, orange, and honey coloured. Also, in less abundance, green, red, violet, and black.

Popular forms: Chips, rounds, rondelles, and nuggets.

Relative cost: ££

Companions: Beautiful with silver and stones that contain hints of the amber colour, such as picture jasper.

THE FACTS:

Amber is an organic material made from fossilized tree resin. It is transparent or translucent and occurs as small masses that may have a rough surface. Sometimes amber contains flies or particles of moss or lichen that were trapped in the resin when it was still sticky, millions of years ago.

Amber has been imitated by a number of man-made materials, such as plastic, glass, and synthetic resin. Some natural resins have also been used to re-create this fascinating material.

Amber is perceived as possessing energies that bring about good fortune, and have the ability to dispel depression and dissolve opposition.

Unakite and amber – page 90

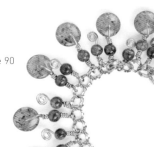

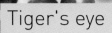

Smoky quartz

Bronzite

Tiger's eye

Typical colours: Brown or black.

Popular forms: Rounds, chips, tubes, and faceted beads, or pendants in a number of shapes.

Relative cost: ££

Companions: Sits well with gold beads or settings, and can be teamed with rose quartz for a softly complementary look, or with pearls for an opulent effect.

THE FACTS:

The colouring of this attractive member of the quartz family is caused by the irradiation of rock crystal containing aluminium. This process may occur naturally or with human intervention. A very dark brown to black variety of this goes by the name of morion.

This transparent quartz lends itself well to being cut and faceted in a number of unusual ways. It has a distinctive appearance and is easily recognized.

Smoky quartz is seen as a grounding stone, and it is believed to bring calm, lift depression, and remove negativity.

Smoky quartz – page 94

Typical colours: Brown ranging to green.

Popular forms: Ovals, teardrops, coins, tubes, and rectangles.

Relative cost: £

Companions: Can be used to dramatic effect with blues and greens, such as malachite or turquoise, and enhanced with silver.

THE FACTS:

Bronzite belongs to the orthopyroxene group of minerals, which are often found in many igneous and metamorphic rocks. It ranges from brown to green in colour and has a metallic lustre when cut. Bronzite displays lots of swirly chocolate patterning and is a very attractive stone, albeit one of the lesser known gemstones.

Along with other gemstones that contain iron, bronzite is seen to have a protective quality, and to have the power to repel any negativity to its source. It is also perceived to help with certainty, to aid with asserting control, and to promote change in an harmonious way.

Typical colours: Yellow, red-brown, and honey colour.

Popular forms: Chips, rounds, ovals, rondelles, and cabochons.

Relative cost: £

Companions: Subtle effects are achieved when combined with creamy colours, such as softly coloured agates. Use with amazonite for a more dramatic style.

THE FACTS:

Tiger's eye is a member of the quartz family, and has a chatoyance – an optical reflectance – that occurs in the fibrous structure of the stone. The best cut to show this chatoyance is as a cabochon.

The natural colour of this stone is yellow to red-brown, although through heat treatments it can change to an attractive deep red colour. Tiger's eye can also be found in a blue variant, sometimes called hawk's eye.

Tiger's eye is a stone used for protection and grounding. It is believed to help with integrity and willpower, and to bring good fortune.

Tiger's eye – page 94

Chrysoberyl

Typical colours: Green, greenish yellow, yellow, and brown.

Popular forms: Rounds, cabochons, ovals, rondelles, and nuggets.

Relative cost: £

Companions: Citrine, silver, and rose quartz.

THE FACTS:

Chrysoberyl takes its name from the Greek *chrysos*, which means "golden", and *beryllos*, for its beryllium content. It appears in a range of colours, from green to yellow and brown and is a durable stone.

Also known as cat's eye, when cut as a cabochon chrysoberyl manifests an almost white line across a yellow-coloured stone. The most valued of these stones is a light golden brown with a shadow providing light and dark tones.

Alexandrite is the other member of the chrysoberyl family, and this is a rare and valuable stone that is green but changes to shades of red, mauve, and brown under artificial light.

Chrysoberyl is seen as a protective stone that can keep disaster at bay. It is also believed that this stone can promote concentration and help with learning.

Picture jasper

Typical colours: Brown, red, yellow, pink tones, and greys.

Popular forms: Rounds, ovals, nuggets, hearts, and faceted cuts.

Relative cost: £

Companions: Peridot or apatite for contrast, or use silver and crystals to add sparkle.

THE FACTS:

Jasper is a chalcedony that is opaque and impure. Picture jasper is one of the best known varieties of jasper, and it takes its name from its landscape patterns and varied colour range.

Picture jasper can be cut into various interesting bead shapes, and its many patterns and colours, influenced by the occurrence of different minerals in the stone, give each piece of jewellery made with it originality and style.

Picture jasper is claimed to bring harmony and proportion, and can be used as an emotional healing stone.

Rhyolite

Typical colours: Brown to reddish or greeny brown and sometimes grey tones, all flecked with browns and tans.

Popular forms: Rounds, coins, hearts, ovals, and rectangles.

Relative cost: £

Companions: Attractive when used with gold or copper findings and gemstone beads in colours that pick out those found within the pattern of the rhyolite.

THE FACTS:

Rhyolite is found in silicon-rich igneous volcanic rock. The many patterns displayed within the cut gemstones have come about through the extensive movement of gases when the rock was being formed.

Rhyolite is said to promote change and creativity, increase self-esteem, and aid in communication.

Rhyolite – page 91

Amber and picture jasper – page 109

Aragonite

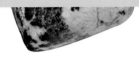

Citrine and ametrine

Yellow turquoise

Typical colours: Usually colourless or white when pure, and translucent or transparent.

Popular forms: Rounds, rondelles, ovals, and carved shapes.

Relative cost: £

Companions: Use with earthy quartzes, onyx, or amber and silver for a subtle style.

THE FACTS:

Aragonite is a naturally occurring mineral, calcium carbonate. It is usually colourless or white when pure but impurities can bring about shades of yellow, blue, pink, or green. It was named after Molina de Aragón in Spain, where it was discovered.

This stone is said to possess energies to aid with grounding, and is believed to be beneficial in connecting us to our past and childhood in a positive way. It is also believed to aid with spinal healing and in the absorption of calcium.

Typical colours: Yellow, orange, or brown.

Popular forms: Briolette, faceted rondelles, nuggets, drops, and chips.

Relative cost: ££

Companions: The yellow and orange forms look stunning when teamed with smoky quartz and either silver or gold.

THE FACTS:

Citrine belongs to the quartz family. A lot of commercially produced citrine is really amethyst or smoky quartz that has been heat-treated to produce a popular orange-yellow citrine.

Ametrine is also very popular. It is created when amethyst is heat-treated to form citrine, then a portion of it is irradiated in order to be converted back to amethyst, resulting in a beautiful, softly coloured half-lilac and half-yellow stone.

Citrine is associated with success and good fortune and is believed to enhance mental clarity, creativity, and willpower.

Typical colours: Yellow, black, brown, and green.

Popular forms: Rounds, chips, ovals, squares, and coins.

Relative cost: £

Companions: The soft variety is striking with purples such as amethyst or jade. Yellow turquoise is also attractive as a standalone stone, accented with silver.

THE FACTS:

There are two types of stone referred to as yellow turquoise. Hard yellow turquoise is a natural stone that is not in fact turquoise, but serpentine. It is chartreuse yellow and black with tinges of brown, green, and red. Soft yellow turquoise is sold as natural turquoise enhanced with dye to achieve a strong yellow colour with a black matrix. In theory, any stone, such as howlite, magnesite, dolomite, or calcite, could be dyed and passed off as real turquoise.

Aragonite – page 101

Citrine – page 102

Unakite

Typical colours: Mottled green and pink.

Popular forms: Rounds, ovals, rondelles, and geometric and carved shapes.

Relative cost: £

Companions: Use pink coral or rhodonite to bring out the pink, with silver to add reflection and lift.

THE FACTS:

Unakite is an altered granite made up of pink feldspar, green epidote, and clear quartz. It has a mottled pink and green colour, polishes well, and can easily be worked into many shapes for beads.

Unakite is very attractive when carved into the shapes of flowers or beads, because the mottled pattern gives real texture to the designs.

Unakite is perceived as a stone useful in the unity of the emotional, mental, and spiritual aspects of a person. It is also believed to possess energies to ensure a healthy reproductive system, and as such is thought to be beneficial when worn or carried by pregnant women.

Ocean jasper

Typical colours: Highly patterned with pink, green, grey, white, and red.

Popular forms: Rounds, barrels, ovals, nuggets, marquise, and free-form shapes.

Relative cost: £

Companions: Silver, pearls, and softly coloured stones like chrysoprase will pick out the colours within the ocean jasper.

THE FACTS:

Ocean jasper is also referred to as orbicular jasper, due to its white or grey-green eye-shaped patterns, surrounded by red jasper. Ocean jasper is actually more of an agate than a jasper, because agate is translucent and jasper is opaque. The jasper part of its name pertains to its similarity to rhyolite, and the fact that Madagascar Minerals list jasper as the mineral resource where it is mined. The ocean part of the name refers to the fact that this mineral is mainly found at the edge of the sea.

Ocean jasper is perceived as a soothing stone that can heal emotions and help us take on responsibility and dispel negativity.

Bloodstone

Typical colours: Green with red inclusions.

Popular forms: Rounds, ovals, nuggets, tubes, and carved beads.

Relative cost: £

Companions: Team with red jasper or carnelian to bring out the red inclusions, and brighten with crystals and silver, or even copper.

THE FACTS:

Also known as heliotrope, bloodstone is a form of chalcedony. The red inclusions in this green jasper are caused by iron oxide or the appearance of red jasper. Sometimes yellow or other colours may be present.

This stone was treasured in ancient times, and was believed to have been formed when the blood of Christ stained some jasper below the cross. It was said to possess miraculous powers and even to enable its wearer to become invisible. Today it is thought to promote circulation in the body and remove energy blockages.

Ocean jasper – page 96

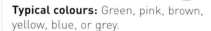

Zoisite

Chrysocolla

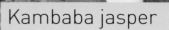

Kambaba jasper

Typical colours: Green, pink, brown, yellow, blue, or grey.

Popular forms: Rounds, nuggets, and faceted shapes.

Relative cost: ££

Companions: Use garnet or rhodonite to enhance the pink or jade to pick out the green. Also looks great with garnet and silver or gold.

THE FACTS:

There are several varieties of zoisite, one is tanzanite, which is highly sought after, then there is thulite, which is pink in colour due to the manganese present. A popular variant is the green type where ruby is present, known as ruby in zoisite, or ruby zoisite. This is a stunning stone to work with due to the swirling mix of green and rich, ruby red. Sometimes it contains black inclusions known as hornblende.

Ruby zoisite is believed to help the wearer bring their creative thoughts to fruition. It is also said to be able to settle obsessive emotions targeted at another person.

Typical colours: Blue-green, sometimes with white streaks.

Popular forms: Rounds, ovals, coins, rondelles, and squares.

Relative cost: £

Companions: Turquoise, labradorite, or lapis lazuli.

THE FACTS:

Chrysocolla is a mineral that forms in the oxidization zones of other copper ore bodies, for example azurite, malachite, cuprite, limonite, and quartz. It is sometimes confused with turquoise due to its light colour.

Chrysocolla is a soft stone so is often stabilized before being made into beads.

Chrysocolla is regarded as having the ability to ease fear, anxiety, and guilt.

Typical colours: Mottled with shades of green, brown, and black.

Popular forms: Rounds, ovals, rectangles, and many faceted shapes.

Relative cost: £

Companions: Looks stunning when complemented with limestone, crystals, and silver.

THE FACTS:

This stone is a member of the quartz family and has a striking appearance. Also known as star galaxy jasper, its patterns of spots and concentric rings in shades of green, black, and brown sometimes look like a galaxy.

Kambaba jasper is regarded as having the energy to stabilize emotions and the dietary system, and help us to connect with the earth's energies.

Ruby in zoisite – page 83

Kambaba jasper and limestone – page 89

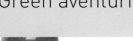

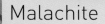

Aventurine

Typical colours: Blue, green, dark green, red, peach, and brown.

Popular forms: Rounds, ovals, coins, and many carved and faceted shapes.

Relative cost: £

Companions: All the colours of aventurine look wonderful with silver, crystals, and glass lampworked beads.

THE FACTS:

Aventurine is a translucent to opaque quartz with glistening mineral inclusions. The red, green, and blue colours of aventurine are caused by the different minerals present, such as chrome fuchsite mica, which displays a green colour, and pyrite or hematite, that cause a brown or orange effect.

Aventurine is seen to be beneficial for mental grounding and to aid with clarity and self-confidence. It is also believed to increase libido.

Lapis lazuli and green aventurine – page 93

Green aventurine

Typical colours: Dark or light green.

Popular forms: Rounds, ovals, hearts, rondelles, and faceted beads in many different shapes.

Relative cost: £

Companions: Use with silver and clear or AB crystals to show off the vibrant green and shimmer of this stone.

THE FACTS:

Aventurine is a member of the quartz family. Although most commonly found in green, it may also manifest as orange to red, brown, yellow, blue, or grey. It is a translucent stone with mineral inclusions that give it a shimmery appearance.

Aventurine is believed to enhance creativity and imagination and promote mental clarity. Green aventurine is said to be a mystical stone of prosperity that can bring friendship into the bearer's life.

Malachite

Typical colours: Green with many shades of green banding within.

Popular forms: Rounds, cabochons, ovals, hearts, and faceted pieces.

Relative cost: ££

Companions: Turquoise, coral, mother-of-pearl, and onyx. Set with silver or copper.

THE FACTS:

Malachite is opaque, found in masses, and takes its colour from its copper content.

This well-known and popular stone has beautifully banded striations in varying shades of green, and can be cut and polished in many ways to enhance this. High-grade, faceted beads can be fairly expensive, but lower grade, more simply cut beads and pendants are just as satisfying to work with and still show off the beautiful patterns in the stone.

Malachite is said to be able to heal the heart and the body. It is believed to have energies helpful for centring and balancing, and thought to bring about prosperity. Using it with copper is said to enhance its power.

Malachite – page 100

Chrysoprase

Typical colours: Apple green.

Popular forms: Rounds, nuggets, and cabochons.

Relative cost: £££

Companions: Beautiful in its simplicity when used with gold.

THE FACTS:

Chrysoprase is a chalcedony and the most valued variety is the translucent apple green type. The colour comes from the presence of nickel.

Fine-grade examples of this stone, without flaws, imperfections, or inclusions, can be very expensive.

Chrysoprase is believed to protect children, animals, or seedlings. It is also said to help with emotions and sexual imbalance.

Chrysoprase and pearl – page 106

Peridot

Typical colours: Yellowy green to olive or bottle green.

Popular forms: Chips, rounds, rondelles, nuggets, and teardrops.

Relative cost: ££

Companions: Striking with tiger's eye or garnet and always lovely with silver.

THE FACTS:

Peridot is the gemstone variant of olivine, and its distinctive bottle or olive green colour is due to the presence of iron. This stone does not need to be treated in any way to enhance its colour.

High-grade, highly polished, and multi-faceted stones or beads can be reasonably expensive but very rewarding to work with, because their reflective surfaces enhance the lovely colour of the peridot. Choosing lower grade, smooth stones will be more budget-friendly and can look equally attractive in jewellery designs.

Peridot is believed to enable the healing and harmony of relationships, in particular marriage, and is said to provide a protective shield around the body of the wearer.

Serpentine

Typical colours: Light or dark green, sometimes with white patches and dark veining.

Popular forms: Tubes, rounds, ovals, chips, and cabochons.

Relative cost: £

Companions: Very attractive with copper and other contrasting colours, such as strawberry quartz.

THE FACTS:

Serpentine refers to a group of green minerals forming intergrown crystals that grow in masses. There are as many as twenty varieties of serpentine in this group.

Serpentine is usually green with a mottled, scaly appearance, and this is what gives it its name, referring to the Latin *serpentinus*, meaning "serpent rock".

This stone is associated with happiness and success, and is believed to promote good luck and enable people to achieve their business and personal goals.

Carnelian, garnet, and peridot – page 89

Aquamarine

Typical colours: Sea green, sky blue, or dark blue.

Popular forms: Rounds, nuggets, rondelles, ovals, and chips.

Relative cost: ££

Companions: Use with dark blues and greens, for example apatite or azurite, to really enhance the colours. Aquamarine looks lovely when used with silver and pearls or mother-of-pearl.

THE FACTS:

Aquamarine is a member of the beryl family. In the nineteenth century the most popular colour was sea green, and the name aquamarine actually means "sea water".

Aquamarine is dichroic, meaning that it appears blue or colourless as the stone is viewed from different angles, and is heat-treated to enhance its colour.

Aquamarine is believed to be a stone of courage, and said to help remove prejudices and break old habits.

Aquamarine and pearl – page 51

Apatite

Typical colours: Yellow, blue, violet, pink, green, or colourless.

Popular forms: Nuggets, chips, coins, and faceted rondelles.

Relative cost: ££

Companions: Turquoise, aquamarine, pearls, and silver.

THE FACTS:

Apatite is a fairly soft phosphate mineral. The chatoyant stones are known as cat's eye apatite, while transparent yellowy green stones are called asparagus stone, and blue stones can be known as moroxite. The cost of the stone increases with the intensity of the colour.

Beads are frequently available as natural, opaque stone, which when polished up as nuggets or tumbled beads, display a rich dark blue with some dark, almost red inclusions, or teal blue with white markings. Translucent apatite crystals can also be cut and faceted and sold as beads such as small rondelles.

This is a particularly soft stone and is easily scratched, so it is best used in necklaces and earrings.

Apatite is believed to reduce appetite and enhance insight and creativity.

Larimar

Typical colours: Light blue, green-blue, deep blue, or white.

Popular forms: Rounds, rondelles, free-form, and nuggets.

Relative cost: £££

Companions: Use with silver and crystals that complement the myriad colours in the larimar.

THE FACTS:

Larimar, sometimes referred to as lorimar, is a rare blue type of pectolite found in the Dominican Republic in the Caribbean. Pectolite is found in other places, but not with the blue of larimar, which is due to the substitution of cobalt for calcium in its composition.

The stone is graded according to coloration, white is the lowest grade, with volcanic blue being the highest. Sky blue to volcanic blue stones are most often used in high-quality jewellery. Larimar may sometimes possess green or red inclusions.

Cutting larimar into beads is a laborious and costly process due to the amount of material lost in the procedure.

Larimar is perceived as a soothing stone and is believed to help ease stress and stimulate brain activity.

Amazonite

Typical colours: Blue to blue-green.

Popular forms: Rounds, chips, coins, nuggets, and faceted beads.

Relative cost: £

Companions: Very attractive when used with smoky quartz, chrysoberyl, or sparkling crystals in complementary colours.

THE FACTS:

Due to the amount of lead present, this attractive, semi-opaque stone is either solid blue-green or pale blue with black, grey, and white markings. Amazonite may also appear showing yellow, red, grey, and pink coloration, but the blue-green variety is most commonly used in jewellery.

Amazonite is believed to help calm the nerves and relieve emotional disturbance.

Blue opal

Typical colours: Blue to blue-green or aqua.

Popular forms: Faceted rondelles, cabochons, and rounds.

Relative cost: £££

Companions: White pearls and silver.

THE FACTS:

Blue opal, also known as Peruvian opal due to its locality, is a semi-opaque or opaque blue-green stone. It is a fairly rare stone and disreputable dealers often attempt to pass dyed stones off as the original opals.

Blue opal can be cut clear and scenic to show variations of colour, or dendritic to show black, fernlike markings.

It is said that blue opal can open the pathways for communication and relieve them of stress. It is also believed to aid restful sleep.

Natural and African turquoise

Typical colours: Green to sky blue.

Popular forms: Rounds, teardrops, rondelles, heishi, ovals, and nuggets.

Relative cost: ££

Companions: Attractive when used with rich purples, such as amethyst or purple crystals, and lovely when teamed with chocolate browns such as smoky quartz or bronzite.

THE FACTS:

Turquoise was one of the first gemstones ever to be mined and is famed for its intense colour, which ranges from green to sky blue. The colour variations are due to the amounts of copper or iron present.

The matrix, or mother rock, where the turquoise was found often forms veining, referred to as "spiderweb matrix". Sometimes this adds value to the stone if it looks particularly good, but this is unusual.

Turquoise is a very light material that is fragile and porous, which can lead to fading and cracking, so it is often treated with wax or resin, which adds stability.

The hardness of the stone and the depth of its colour are what determine its value. In most cases the more desirable colours range from sky blue to a robin-egg blue.

Turquoise is believed to be a stone of communication, and is recommended for public speakers. It is also regarded as helpful in relieving sadness or grief.

Blue opal – page 81

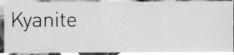

Howlite

Typical colours: Usually dyed many different colours, most often to resemble turquoise, but naturally white or grey.

Popular forms: Rounds, rondelles, ovals, heishi, and geometric shapes.

Relative cost: £

Companions: Use howlite dyed to resemble turquoise as for true turquoise. Natural white howlite can be teamed with natural chrysoberyl to enhance the grey veining, or, for extra drama, team it with any brightly coloured stone, such as malachite or rhodonite.

THE FACTS:

This stone is famous for being dyed to impersonate other gemstones, especially turquoise or lapis lazuli. It is not a particularly hard stone, but it is durable and will polish up extremely well.

Natural howlite is snow white in colour with fine grey or black veins, often forming a weblike pattern.

Howlite is believed to teach patience to its bearer and aid in absorbing anger, whether it be your own or directed at you from a third party.

Kyanite and pearls – page 61

Kyanite

Typical colours: Blue, grey, white, or green.

Popular forms: Sticks, rectangles, and nuggets.

Relative cost: ££

Companions: Pearls, moonstone, and silver contrast well with kyanite.

THE FACTS:

Kyanite takes its name from the Greek *kyanos*, which means "blue". It is a translucent bluish grey stone that has a metallic sheen.

Kyanite is one of the stones that has a variable hardness according to whether it is cut across or lengthways on a cleavage plane. Because of this it is rarely faceted and instead, usually polished smooth and set in jewellery or sold in the rough.

Kyanite is believed to be beneficial in improving communication, alleviating confusion, and aiding intuition.

Azurite

Typical colours: Intense blue with other shades of blue, green, and sometimes red running through.

Popular forms: Rounds, heishi, and ovals.

Relative cost: ££

Companions: Malachite, lapis lazuli, amazonite, and turquoise.

THE FACTS:

Azurite is an azure blue copper mineral produced by the weathering of deposits of copper ore, occasionally found as prismatic crystals but more commonly in masses where it is intergrown with malachite, chrysocolla, or turquoise.

Azurite is quite a soft stone and heat, bright light, and exposure to the air can all cause it to lose its colour, so it should be sealed and stored carefully in the dark. It is sometimes coated with wax or hardened for stability.

Azurite is believed to improve psychic ability and bring on prophetic dreams. It is also said to improve creativity.

Azurite and malachite – page 101

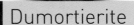

Blue tiger's eye

Blue goldstone

Dumortierite

Typical colours: Blue, blue-black, grey, or green.

Popular forms: Rounds and discs.

Relative cost: £

Companions: Striking with gold or copper, and complemented beautifully by brown tiger's eye.

THE FACTS:

Blue tiger's eye – or hawk's eye – is a chatoyant gemstone that forms when quartz gets embedded in a fibrous mineral called crocidolite. Tiger's eye is usually reddish brown, but the blue type occurs when traces of iron oxide are deposited in the crocidolite. The amount of iron oxide determines the depth of the blue coloration. Brown tiger's eye and blue tiger's eye therefore have slightly different internal structures.

Tiger's eye is believed to be helpful for health and well-being, perception, insight, and courage.

Typical colours: Very dark blue with copper-coloured sparkle.

Popular forms: Rounds, rondelles, ovals, tubes, and hearts.

Relative cost: £

Companions: Fantastic with copper, gold, or silver, especially when combined with a stone such as lapis lazuli or sodalite.

THE FACTS:

Blue goldstone is a man-made stone sometimes mistaken for a naturally occurring mineral, and is formed by adding copper salts to glass in a furnace. Dye is added to give the rich blue colour, and the copper is suspended in the glass, giving a wonderful sparkle.

Using blue goldstone in jewellery gives an exotic or celestial feel and stunning effects.

Blue goldstone is said to be a stone of wisdom and science. It is believed to help lift depression and reduce anxiety.

Typical colours: Violet-blue, reddish brown, and red.

Popular forms: Rondelles, heishi, nuggets, rounds, and tubes.

Relative cost: £

Companions: Dumortierite suits designs with azurite or lapis lazuli and is lovely set with gold or rich yellow gold vermeil.

THE FACTS:

Dumortierite is a borosilicate mineral with attractive, bright colouring. It is a hard, durable stone and is popular for ornamental use.

Dumortierite is sometimes mistaken for lapis lazuli and is referred to as the blue denim stone. It looks great worn with jeans and is ideal for men's jewellery.

This stone is thought to help the wearer gain control over his life and is believed to be helpful in the treatment of compulsive or addictive disorders.

Dumortierite and blue goldstone – page 81

Sodalite

Blue coral

Lapis lazuli

Typical colours: All shades of blue, sometimes with white markings.

Popular forms: Rounds, tubes, coins, rondelles, chips, and faceted shapes.

Relative cost: £

Companions: Lapis lazuli and hematite look good with sodalite, especially when matched with silver.

THE FACTS:

Sodalite – so called for its sodium content – is found in many shades of blue, often with streaks of white calcite, and can be carved for use in jewellery. It may also be grey, yellow, pink, or green, but it is the blue variant that is used for jewellery.

Sodalite is perceived as having the power to increase confidence, enhance creativity, and alleviate fear.

Sodalite – page 70

Typical colours: Soft denim blue.

Popular forms: Chips, heishi, and rounds.

Relative cost: ££

Companions: Red coral, mother-of-pearl, and silver.

THE FACTS:

Blue ridge coral and denim coral grow in the Indo-Pacific region and are now quite hard to find. They are a soft denim blue in colour, porous, and often lacquered. Blue coral is believed to be coral that is starting to decay, because the blue sections are found at the tips or on the surface.

Blue sponge coral is more easily found and much more affordable than the denim and blue ridge corals. It is a more dense material and the cavities are less visible.

Sea bamboo or bamboo coral has sections of branchlike calcium carbonate with regions of gorgonin protein at the joints. Its natural colour is creamy white with brown or black markings. It is lighter than natural corals and is often dyed blue and sold as one of the naturally blue corals.

Typical colours: Intense blue with patches of white or brassy yellow.

Popular forms: Rounds, rectangles, chips, discs, rondelles, and nuggets.

Relative cost: ££

Companions: Stunning with copper or gold and teamed with bright colours, such as carnelian and turquoise, for an ancient Egyptian theme.

THE FACTS:

Lapis lazuli is a blue rock that comprises different minerals, including lazurite, sodalite, hauyne, calcite, and pyrite. The best quality lapis lazuli is an intense blue with small flecks of yellow pyrite.

Lapis lazuli has been imitated using stained jasper or paste with copper. Another imitation uses a high percentage of lazurite. Lower grade lapis is often dyed to enhance its colour in an attempt to emulate the more expensive stones, however this often results in a dark stone with a noticeable grey cast.

Lapis lazuli is said to enhance awareness and intellect, and is believed to impart ancient knowledge and wisdom.

Turquoise and lapis lazuli – page 79

Amethyst

Iolite

Tanzanite

Typical colours: Varying shades of purple from lavender or rose to rich magenta.

Popular forms: Rounds, chips, drops, pendants, nuggets, and faceted beads.

Relative cost: ££

Companions: Silver, sparkling crystals, glass beads or soft-toned rose quartz.

Typical colours: Sapphire blue, blue-violet, yellowy grey, or light blue.

Popular forms: Chips, flat ovals, or coins, and many faceted shapes.

Relative cost: ££

Companions: Pretty with blue topaz, pearls, and silver.

Typical colours: Blue-purple to ultramarine.

Popular forms: Chips, ovals, rondelles, and faceted beads.

Relative cost: ££

Companions: Pink tourmaline, clear crystals, and gold or silver.

THE FACTS:

Amethyst is crystalline quartz appearing in all shades of mauve, purple, or lilac. It is dichroic and shows tints of blue or reddish purple when viewed from different angles.

Lower grade amethyst is often tumbled to make beads. Deep Siberian amethyst is quite rare and considered to be the premium grade of stone. It has a strong purple hue with secondary tones of blue and red.

Amethyst is perceived as a symbol of heavenly awareness and is said to calm and clear the mind.

THE FACTS:

Iolite is the transparent gemstone variant of cordierite. The name comes from the Greek *ios*, which means "violet". Violet-blue iolite has sometimes been referred to as water sapphire, due to the similarity in colour to blue sapphire.

Iolite is commonly dyed to enhance its appearance.

This stone is believed to open up the spiritual pathways and aid with connecting to the "higher self". It is said to aid the bearer in letting go of unwanted patterns and to introduce positive energy into life.

THE FACTS:

Tanzanite is a variant of the mineral zoisite and is a blueish purple in colour. It was discovered in Tanzania, hence it's name.

An extremely popular gemstone, it is often heat-treated to enhance its colour. The large deep blue crystals are becoming increasingly scarce, generally only smaller grains are found. Paler coloured stones are more abundant and are faceted and used for beads.

Tanzanite is considered to be helpful with change. It is also said to be an uplifting stone that can help with encouraging happy and compassionate feelings.

Amethyst and peridot – page 84

Iolite – page 84

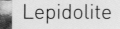

Charoite

Lepidolite

Blue lace agate

Typical colours: Lavender, violet, lilac, or dark purple.

Popular forms: Rondelles, barrels, ovals, and cabochons.

Relative cost: £££

Companions: Stunning as a standalone enhanced only by gold or silver, or teamed with pearls.

Typical colours: Violet, white, or pale pink to salmon coloured, sometimes with grey or yellow running through.

Popular forms: Rounds, ovals, coins, and rectangles.

Relative cost: £

Companions: Amethyst, silver, moonstone, and pale blue quartz.

Typical colours: Very pale blue with delicate white banding.

Popular forms: Rounds, ovals, coins, nuggets, and faceted shapes.

Relative cost: ££

Companions: Mother-of-pearl, silver, and crystals of many colours, including shades of blue or pink.

THE FACTS:

Charoite was reported to be discovered in Russia in the 1940s, but was not known to the outside world until 1978. It is only found in the Sakha Republic in Siberia.

This translucent stone with its fibrous, swirly characteristics occurs in many shades of lilac and purple, and sometimes displays black, transparent, or orange patterns. High-grade stones are costly because it is quite rare, and there are some export restrictions placed upon it.

This stone is believed to enhance self-esteem and promote spiritual growth.

THE FACTS:

Lepidolite is a mineral – called mica – so will sometimes display a sparkly appearance. It is a flexible material found in igneous rocks and also in veins with tin.

The soft colouring of lepidolite is natural and does not require enhancement with any treatments.

Lepidolite is said to encourage independence. It is also said to help with concentration, prevent distraction, and act as an aid to restful sleep.

THE FACTS:

Blue lace agate is a variegated chalcedony that displays clearly defined coloured bands or markings.

Blue lace agate has become a very popular stone, but the amount mined each year is lessening. If new deposits are not found in the future, the stone risks extinction.

Blue lace agate is believed to be a stone of tranquillity, and is said to lessen anger and calm nervousness.

Charoite – page 102

Rhodonite

Typical colours: Rose pink to orangey red, sometimes black.

Popular forms: Chips, coins, ovals, rounds, nuggets, rondelles, and carved focals.

Relative cost: £

Companions: Great with other warm colours, such as the pinks and purples of amethyst or rose quartz. Also works well with complementary green tones, so some of the jaspers can be used here.

THE FACTS:

Rhodonite is a manganese silicate and a member of the pyroxene group of minerals found in many igneous and metamorphic rocks. Ranging from pale pink to orangey red, rhodonite can also carry a strong black matrix that looks absolutely stunning in jewellery pieces.

Rhodonite lends itself very well to being fashioned into many bead shapes or carved into focal pieces.

This stone is said to represent inner balance, to help with self-confidence, and to have a calming effect on the nervous system.

Tourmaline – page 83

Tourmaline

Typical colours: Black, brown, clear, pink, red, green, and yellow.

Popular forms: Rondelles, nuggets, ovals, and faceted shapes.

Relative cost: ££

Companions: Silver, gold, and glass in complementary colours.

THE FACTS:

Tourmaline refers to a group of similar minerals that manifest many colours. Schorl is the most abundant of the tourmaline group. It is iron-rich, opaque, and black in colour. Dravite is a dark brown tourmaline that can be lightened with treatment. Indicolite refers to the dark blue tourmaline that can be heat-treated to lighten the colour. Rubellite is the name given to the highly prized red stones. Watermelon tourmalines are reminiscent of the fruit because they are made up of pink crystals with a green rim, or vice versa.

Yellow-green is the most common colour for tourmaline, with the emerald shades being the most rare and valuable.

Fluorite

Typical colours: Yellow, pink, purple, blue, and green.

Popular forms: Rounds, coins, rectangles, pebbles, and heishi.

Relative cost: £

Companions: Silver, glass crystals, amethyst, and lepidolite.

THE FACTS:

Fluorite is quite a soft stone, but it has such a range of natural colours, often occurring within the same specimen, that it really is a lovely stone to work with.

The most common shades of fluorite used for beads are golden, green, purple, and rainbow.

Fluorite is said to enhance concentration and aid impartiality and reasoning. It is also believed to help dispel negativity.

Moss agate

Snowflake obsidian

Pyrite

Typical colours: White with green inclusions.

Popular forms: Carved leaves and flowers, nuggets, rounds, and ovals.

Relative cost: £

Companions: Use with earthy toned jaspers and agates, or bronzite, for a natural, earthy feel.

THE FACTS:

Moss agate is sometimes referred to as mocha stone. It is made from silicon dioxide and commonly found in granite and limestone. The patterns formed within by mineral deposits resemble moss.

Because of its markings, moss agate has been perceived as having a particularly special relationship with nature. It is considered a good stone for those involved with botany or agriculture and is believed to aid bonding with "nature spirits". It is also used to refresh the soul and reveal the beauty of nature.

Typical colours: Black, grey, dark green, and red.

Popular forms: Rounds, cabochons, and pendants.

Relative cost: £

Companions: Looks stunning with silver and coloured crystals.

THE FACTS:

Obsidian is a type of naturally occurring glass that forms as an extrusive igneous rock. Although it is like a mineral, because it is a glass, it lacks a crystalline structure and is therefore not a true mineral.

Snowflake obsidian inherits its pattern due to the occurrence of small, white, clustered crystals of cristobalite.

Believed to be a stone of purity, it is thought that snowflake obsidian draws hidden imbalances to the surface and has healing properties to aid detoxification.

Typical colours: Dark brassy yellow.

Popular forms: Rounds, ovals, rectangles, coins, and nuggets.

Relative cost: £

Companions: Ideal with bold colours such as lapis lazuli, malachite, or turquoise and looks sumptuous with richly coloured stones like amethyst.

THE FACTS:

Pyrite, also known as fool's gold, is an iron sulfide mineral that occurs either as cubes or as pyritohedra with twelve faces, each with a pentagonal edge.

Pyrite has a brassy yellow colour and requires careful cutting because it is quite brittle. It has been used in jewellery for thousands of years and is now mainly used in costume jewellery.

Said to be a stone of great protection, pyrite can be worn or carried when undertaking something dangerous. It is also believed to trigger creative thoughts and aid memory.

Snowflake obsidian –
page 52

Pyrite and turquoise –
page 92

Chapter two
THE DIRECTORY

In this chapter, beautiful examples of jewellery are "deconstructed" so you can see the exact type and quantity of bead that goes into each piece and then re-create them. Or use this chapter as a source of inspiration to make your own unique combinations.

Project Selector

Page 61

Page 62

Page 63

Page 64

Page 65

Page 66

Page 67

Page 68

Page 69

Page 70

Page 71

Page 72

Page 73

Page 74

Page 75

Page 86

Page 87

Page 87

Page 88

Page 88

Page 89

Page 89

Page 90

Page 91

Page 91

Page 92

Page 92

Page 93

Page 94

Page 94

Page 95

Page 95

Page 96

Page 96

Page 97

Page 98

Page 99

Page 99

Earrings

Page 100

Page 100

Page 100

Page 101

Page 101

Page 101

Page 101

Page 102

Page 102

Page 102

Page 103

Page 103

Page 103

Sets

Page 104

Page 105

Page 106

Page 107

Page 108

Page 109

Accessories

Page 110

Page 110

Page 111

Page 111

Page 111

Necklaces

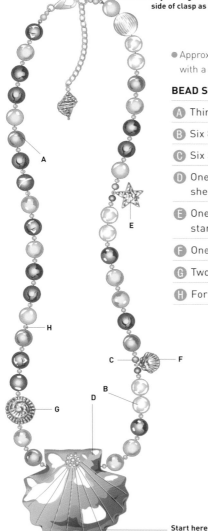

Adjust length from either side of clasp as required.

Start here

- Approximate length 45.5cm (18in.) with a 5cm (2in.) extender

BEAD STORE

Ⓐ Thirty-three 8mm green moss quartz beads

Ⓑ Six 8mm top-drilled white freshwater pearls

Ⓒ Six 3–3.5mm apatite rounds

Ⓓ One 50mm Karen hill tribe silver shell pendant

Ⓔ One 12mm Karen hill tribe silver starfish charm

Ⓕ One 10mm Karen hill tribe silver clam charm

Ⓖ Two 15mm Karen hill tribe silver shell beads

Ⓗ Forty 2mm sterling silver rounds

You will also need:

- Stringing material
- Sterling silver 12mm lobster clasp
- 5-cm (2-in.) length of sterling silver extender chain
- Two sterling silver calottes

Moss quartz and pearl

Karin Chilton ~ Aegean Sea

This stunning necklace would be the perfect accessory for a summer wardrobe or a beach holiday. The multi-toned green moss quartz has a calming colour reminiscent of the sea, and the use of pearls and silver seashells ties the sea theme together.

Aquamarine and pearl

Karen Tan ~ Neptune's Realm

This necklace is a real work of art. It has so many elements to it, but all in perfect harmony. The aquamarine and frosted glass rondelles portray the colour of the sea, while the peacock pearls and seashells allude to the natural sea life. Sea-themed silver charms complete the piece, which has an air of fantasy glamour.

Adjust length from either side of clasp as required.

Start here

You will also need:

- 19-strand Beadalon wire
- 12mm Thai silver fishhook clasp
- Two 7mm sterling silver calottes
- Two 2x2mm sterling silver crimp beads
- Twelve sterling silver jump rings
- 7.5-cm (3-in.) length of silver-plated extender chain
- 5-cm (2-in.) length of 0.6mm (22-gauge) sterling silver wire for wrapping charm at clasp

- Approximate length 38cm (15in.)

BEAD STORE

A Eleven 5x7mm aquamarine rondelles

B Six 7x22mm peacock biwa pearls

C Six 5mm peacock round pearls

D Six 6x8mm frosted glass rondelles

E Five 20mm seashells

F Seven assorted 20mm sea-themed silver-plated charms

G Fifteen 4mm Swarovski bicones in assorted shades of blue

H Sixteen 1x5mm Thai silver spacer discs

I Fourteen 2mm Thai silver seed beads

J Eight 5mm Thai silver coil beads

K Five 2-hole silver-plated spacer bars

L Eight 14mm silver tube beads

Snowflake obsidian

Kim Gover ~ Winter Skies

The snowflake obsidian used in this piece brings to mind a winter's night sky with the snow falling thickly. The striking pendant has dictated the formation of the necklace: the coins have been used to echo the central gemstone and the bright blue crystals highlight the bezel-set stones.

Adjust length from either side of clasp as required.

B

G

C

E

F

D

Start here

The pendant is designed to rest on the central blackstone round.

A

● Approximate length 43cm (17in.)

BEAD STORE

Ⓐ One 65mm (2½in.) snowflake obsidian pendant

Ⓑ Six 15mm snowflake obsidian coins

Ⓒ Fourteen 8mm blackstone rounds

Ⓓ Seven 6mm blackstone rounds

Ⓔ Sixteen 6mm Swarovski indicolite bicones

Ⓕ Twelve 4mm Swarovski indicolite bicones

Ⓖ Six 6mm sterling silver filigree beads

You will also need:

● Beading wire
● Silver toggle clasp
● Two 2x2mm sterling silver crimp beads
● Two 3mm sterling silver crimp covers
● Two 3mm sterling silver spacers

Kyanite, sodalite, and moonstone

Karen Tan ~ Indulgence

What a statement piece this necklace is, with the colours and shapes of the gemstones complementing each other perfectly. The soft blue of the kyanite is a great counterpart for the denim-coloured sodalite, while the moonstone picks out the striations in the darker beads. The addition of the flowers really adds character.

A

B

C

I

H

E

G

D

F

Start by wrapping the three flower charms, then commence stringing from the centre.

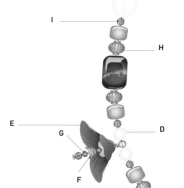

- Approximate length 48cm (19in.)

BEAD STORE

A Six 18x13mm sodalite flat rectangles

B Twelve 7x10mm kyanite rectangles

C Four 18x13mm moonstone ovals

D Six 6mm moonstone rounds

E Three 35mm brown acrylic tri-petal flowers

F Three 6–8mm Czech glass flowers

G Six blue seed beads

H Ten 8mm copper melon beads

I Seventeen 4mm copper filigree beads

You will also need:

- 19-strand Beadalon wire
- Two copper 10mm trigger clasps
- Two 2x2mm sterling silver crimp beads
- Two 7mm copper calottes
- Two 5mm copper jump rings
- Three 5cm (2in.) copper head pins to wrap the flower charms

Bronzite and picture jasper

Gaile Almrott ~ Cave Man

This excellent example of jewellery for men uses earth-toned beads. The rich bronzite draws the eye and is well balanced with the bamboo tubes and the picture jasper buttons, which unite the colours perfectly. The mixture of bead shapes also adds texture and weight to the piece.

Adjust length from either side of clasp as required.

Start here

A

B

C

D

● Approximate length 47.5cm (18¾in.)

BEAD STORE

Ⓐ Five 12mm bronzite squares

Ⓑ Eighteen 8mm picture jasper buttons

Ⓒ Twelve 15x5mm bamboo tubes

Ⓓ Twenty-four 2mm faceted sterling silver spacers

You will also need:

● Beading wire
● Karen hill tribe silver hook clasp
● Two 2x2mm sterling silver crimp beads
● Two 3mm sterling silver crimp covers

● Approximate length 45.5cm (18in.)

BEAD STORE

A Seven 20x10mm fire agate barrel beads

B Fourteen 8mm faceted fire agate beads

C Twenty-eight 6mm fire agate rounds

D Six 6x10mm gold vermeil ornate tubes

E Twelve 8mm gold vermeil disc spacers

You will also need:

● Beading wire
● Gold vermeil hook clasp
● Two 2x2mm gold crimp beads
● Two gold-filled crimp covers
● Four 6mm gold-filled rings

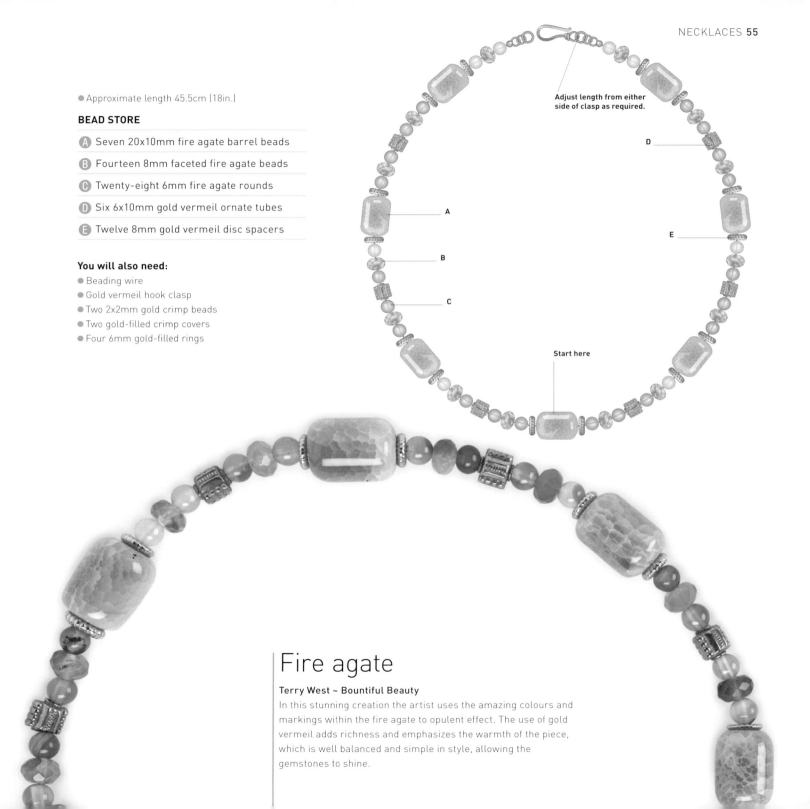

Adjust length from either
side of clasp as required.

D

A

B

C

E

Start here

Fire agate

Terry West ~ Bountiful Beauty

In this stunning creation the artist uses the amazing colours and
markings within the fire agate to opulent effect. The use of gold
vermeil adds richness and emphasizes the warmth of the piece,
which is well balanced and simple in style, allowing the
gemstones to shine.

Opal and Botswana agate

Karin Chilton ~ Sugared Almonds

The soft pink opals forming the focal point of this piece really do have the appearance of sugared almonds, and are greatly enhanced by the grey striped Botswana agate. The combination of diamonds and rounds is very pleasing to the eye and the style is extremely wearable.

● Approximate length 48cm (19in.)

BEAD STORE

Ⓐ Seven 18mm pink opal diamond beads

Ⓑ Thirty-two 8mm Botswana agate rounds

Ⓒ Forty 2mm sterling silver rounds

You will also need:

● Stringing material
● Karen hill tribe silver rose clasp
● Two sterling silver calottes

Adjust length from either side of clasp as required.

Start here

C

B

A

Moss agate and rhodochrosite

Sherril Olive ~ Mossy Bank

This fabulous long-line necklace has been created using lovely moss agate ovals, which have a deep colour and subtle pattern. The contrasting rhodochrosite rounds range in tone from pale pink to light plum, and their colour is enhanced by the addition of bright green crystals. This is a lovely, substantial piece with a great quantity of gemstones.

● Approximate length 80cm (31½in.)

BEAD STORE

(A) Nine 38–40mm moss agate hollow ovals

(B) Twenty-one 10mm rhodochrosite rounds

(C) Twenty-four 8mm rhodochrosite rounds

(D) Twenty-one 4mm Swarovski chrysolite bicones

(E) 2g of size 11 gold or silver Miyuki Delicas

You will also need:

● 100-cm (39-in.) length of Soft Flex beading wire, doubled
● Sterling silver "S" clasp
● Two 2x2mm sterling silver crimp beads

Adjust length from either side of clasp as required.

B

C

A

Start stringing from the central oval.

D

E

Lapis lazuli

Kim Gover ~ Pharaoh's Kiss

This fascinating necklace has an air of ancient Egypt. It has been created with lovely lapis lazuli rectangular beads and blue goldstone round beads – each bead separated by copper spacer beads and copper round beads. The wonderful blue goldstone and copper pendant, and the copper toggle clasp bring harmony to the finished necklace.

- Approximate length 44cm (17⅓in.)

BEAD STORE

- (A) Twenty-two 7x10mm lapis lazuli rectangular beads
- (B) Eight 8mm blue goldstone round beads
- (C) Sixteen 3mm copper round beads
- (D) Fourteen 5mm copper flower spacer beads
- (E) One blue goldstone and copper pendant, approximately 2.5x3cm (1x1¼in.)

You will also need:
- Copper 12mm toggle clasp
- Beading wire
- 2x2mm copper crimp beads
- 3mm copper crimp covers

Adjust length from either side of clasp as required.

Start here

Lepidolite and amethyst

Karin Chilton ~ Parma Violets

This attractive necklace contains myriad purple tones, represented by the lovely muted lilacs and lavenders of the lepidolite and the rich, deep, juicy amethyst. The focal point of the necklace incorporates large lepidolite teardrops enhanced by clusters of amethyst, and the mix of bead shapes adds interest and depth. The artist has included exactly the right amount of silver accent for brightness.

Adjust length from either side of clasp as required.

F
B
C
E
D
A
Start here

● Approximate length 39cm (15½in.) plus the 5cm (2in.) extender

BEAD STORE

Ⓐ Five 20mm lepidolite flat drop side-drilled beads

Ⓑ Thirty 6mm lepidolite rounds

Ⓒ Ten 6mm amethyst rounds

Ⓓ Twelve 8x3mm faceted amethyst side-drilled briolettes

Ⓔ Two 5mm Karen hill tribe silver spiral beads

Ⓕ Forty-two 4mm Bali sterling silver daisy spacers

You will also need:

● Stringing material
● Sterling silver 10mm trigger clasp
● Two sterling silver calottes
● Two 6mm sterling silver jump rings
● 5-cm (2-in.) length of sterling silver extender chain

Blue coral and lava stone

Gaile Almrott ~ It's a Man Thing

Designed with a man in mind, this necklace could be worn with denim or a crisp collared shirt. It is rich in texture with the coral heishi and lava stone beads providing a very organic feel, and the artist has added just the right amount of silver for overall brightness.

● Approximate length 45.5cm (18in.)

BEAD STORE

Ⓐ Sixty-six 5–6mm blue coral heishi beads

Ⓑ Three 10mm lava stone beads

Ⓒ Four 6mm Karen hill tribe silver beads

Ⓓ Fourteen 6mm Karen hill tribe silver discs

Ⓔ Ninety-six 3mm Karen hill tribe silver bicones

You will also need:

● Beading wire
● Silver hook clasp
● Two 2x2mm sterling silver crimp beads
● Two 3mm sterling silver crimp covers

Start here, then adjust length from either side of clasp as required.

Adjust length
from either
side of clasp
as required.

A

B

C

Start here

Kyanite and pearls

Karin Chilton ~ Pacific Seas

Simple in design but very striking, the artist has used kyanite marquise-shaped beads to create amazing texture and movement in this piece. The colours are reminiscent of the sea, from green to pale aqua, and the sea theme is further reinforced with the use of the pearls as accent beads.

● Approximate length 47cm (18½in.)

BEAD STORE

Ⓐ One 40.5-cm (16-in.) string of 11x4mm kyanite marquise beads

Ⓑ Sixteen 6mm freshwater white button-shaped pearls

Ⓒ Thirty-two 2mm sterling silver rounds

You will also need:
● Stringing material
● Karen hill tribe silver 12mm toggle clasp
● Two sterling silver calottes

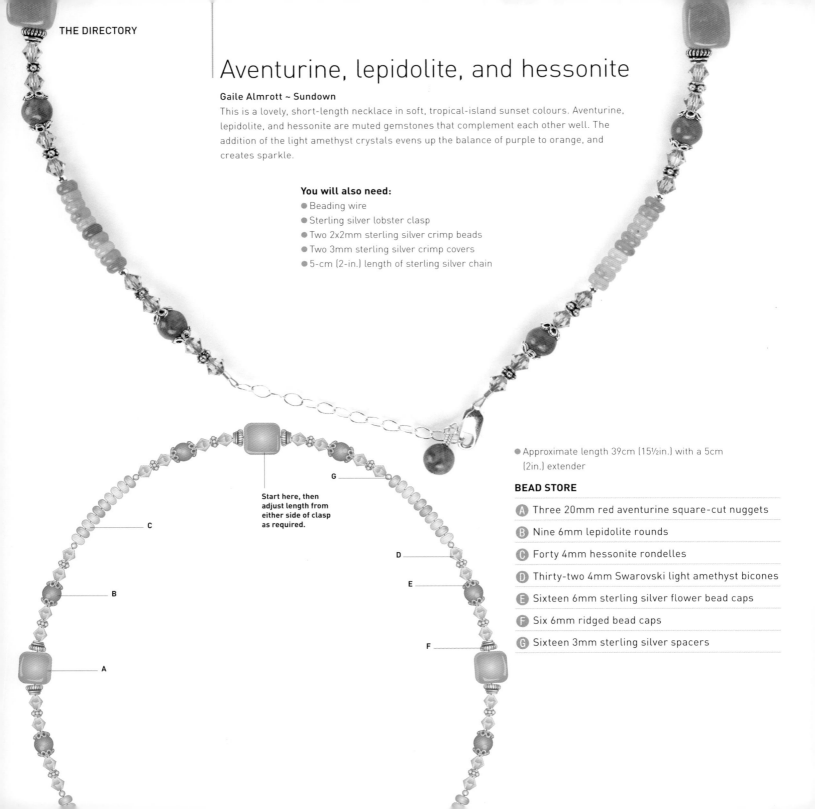

Aventurine, lepidolite, and hessonite

Gaile Almrott ~ Sundown

This is a lovely, short-length necklace in soft, tropical-island sunset colours. Aventurine, lepidolite, and hessonite are muted gemstones that complement each other well. The addition of the light amethyst crystals evens up the balance of purple to orange, and creates sparkle.

You will also need:

- Beading wire
- Sterling silver lobster clasp
- Two 2x2mm sterling silver crimp beads
- Two 3mm sterling silver crimp covers
- 5-cm (2-in.) length of sterling silver chain

Start here, then adjust length from either side of clasp as required.

- Approximate length 39cm (15½in.) with a 5cm (2in.) extender

BEAD STORE

A Three 20mm red aventurine square-cut nuggets

B Nine 6mm lepidolite rounds

C Forty 4mm hessonite rondelles

D Thirty-two 4mm Swarovski light amethyst bicones

E Sixteen 6mm sterling silver flower bead caps

F Six 6mm ridged bead caps

G Sixteen 3mm sterling silver spacers

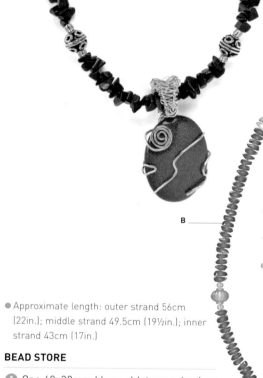

Goldstone

Heather Marrow ~ Dark Alchemy

This is an opulent, mysterious piece of jewellery that is perfect for adding drama to an outfit. The artist has teamed a beautiful dark goldstone cabochon and chips with copper wire, creating warmth and a lavish effect. The three strands are well balanced, with the gradation of colour ranging from the dark outer strand to the lightly beaded inner strand.

Create all the components first. Start by stringing the outer strand from the centre, then construct and attach the inner strands.

● Approximate length: outer strand 56cm (22in.); middle strand 49.5cm (19½in.); inner strand 43cm (17in.)

BEAD STORE

Ⓐ One 40x30mm blue goldstone cabochon

Ⓑ One-hundred-and-twenty blue goldstone chips

Ⓒ Two 12mm Bali-style copper fancy beads

Ⓓ Three 10x12mm Bali-style copper fluted beads

Ⓔ Two 6mm copper daisy spacers

Ⓕ Sixty-six 10/0 teaberry rocaille beads

Ⓖ Two 4x8mm mauve glass rondelles

You will also need:

For the longest strand
● Stringing material
● Two 2x2mm copper crimp beads

For the pendant
● One 1-m (3-ft) length of 1mm (18-gauge) copper wire
● One 3-m (10-ft) length of 0.5mm (24-gauge) copper wire

For the middle strand
● Twenty-eight 9mm (⅓in.) 1mm (18-gauge) copper jump rings
● Eighty 2.5mm (⅒in.) 0.8mm (20-gauge) copper jump rings

For the shortest strand
● Two 9mm (⅓in.) 1mm (18-gauge) copper jump rings
● Twenty-six 9mm (⅓in.) 1mm (18-gauge) copper jump rings
● Ten 10-cm (4in.) lengths of 0.8mm (20-gauge) copper wire

For the three-to-one connectors
● Two 9-cm (3½-in.) lengths of 1mm (18-gauge) copper wire

For the "S" clasp
● One 14-cm (5½-in.) length of 1mm (18-gauge) copper wire
● One 9-cm (3½-in.) length of 0.8mm (20-gauge) copper wire
● 9mm (⅓in.) 1mm (18-gauge) copper jump ring
● Four 4mm (⅛in.) 1mm (18-gauge) copper jump rings

For the extender chain and fob
● Two 9mm (⅓in.) 1mm (18-gauge) copper jump rings
● Four 9mm (⅓in.) 1mm (18-gauge) copper jump rings
● One 5cm (2in.) 0.7mm (21-gauge) copper head pin

Labradorite

Kim Gover ~ Anastasia

This piece is reminiscent of jewellery worn by Russian princesses, featuring faceted labradorite ovals that present wonderful green-blue flashes of colour as the light hits them. This substantial necklace uses copious amounts of crystals and silver to provide a sophisticated spray effect across the décolleté.

● Approximate length 43cm (17in.)

BEAD STORE

Ⓐ Seven faceted labradorite ovals (graduated in size)

Ⓑ Sixteen 8mm Swarovski Montana rounds

Ⓒ Fourteen 6mm Swarovski Montana bicones

Ⓓ Forty-two 4mm Swarovski Montana bicones

Ⓔ Eight 8mm Bali silver flower beads

Ⓕ Thirty-two 6mm rope spacers

Ⓖ Fourteen sterling silver eye pins

Ⓗ Forty-two sterling silver head pins

Ⓘ Fourteen 5mm sterling silver closed jump rings

Ⓙ Eighteen 3mm sterling silver rounds

You will also need:
● Beading wire
● Karen hill tribe silver floral "S" clasp
● Two 2x2mm sterling silver crimp beads

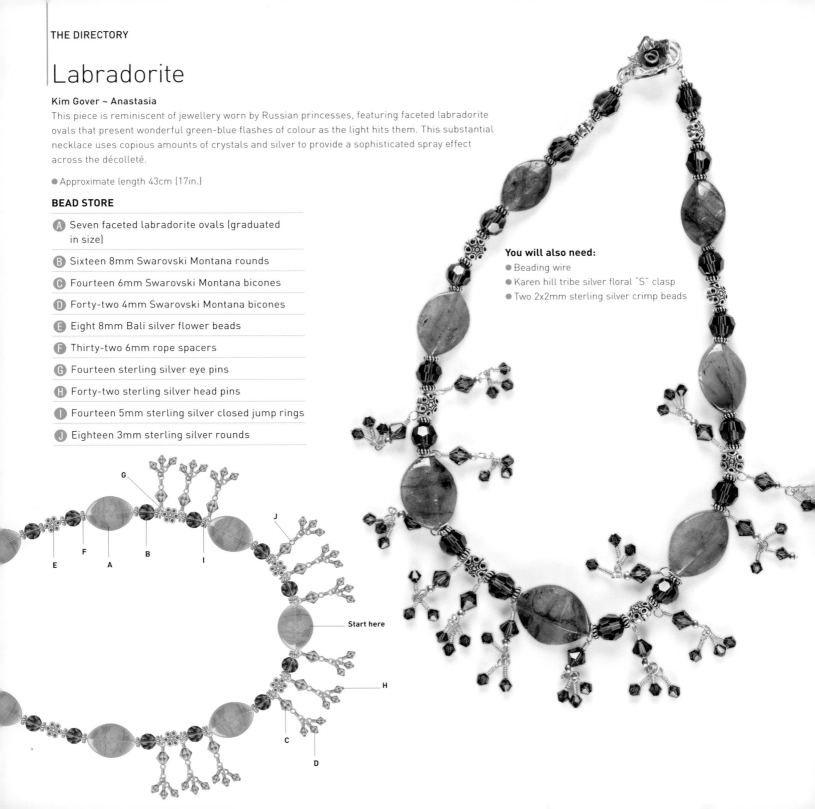

Start here

Hematite

Nan Fry ~ Forest

The focal piece of this necklace has been strung in a very novel way, with the hematite heart appearing suspended between the two wires. There is a large quantity of hematite here, but it has been very well balanced with the large green lampworked beads, and the finished article is irresistible.

Start here using two lengths of wire.

- Approximate length 40cm (16in.)

BEAD STORE

(A) Twenty-two 6mm hematite rounds

(B) Twenty-four 4mm hematite rounds

(C) Fifty-four size 10 hematite glass beads

(D) One hematite heart

(E) Nine green lampworked beads.

You will also need:
- Beading wire
- Silver toggle clasp
- Two 2x2mm sterling silver crimp beads
- Two 3mm sterling silver crimp covers

● Approximate length 46cm (18in.)

BEAD STORE

Ⓐ Two 40mm zebra jasper wavy ovals

Ⓑ One 35mm bamboo jasper teardrop

Ⓒ One 30mm white agate heart

Ⓓ One 25mm white agate wavy oval

Ⓔ Fourteen 6mm white howlite rounds

Ⓕ Two 45–50mm lava stone hollow rectangles

Ⓖ Nine 6mm Swarovski jet bicones

Ⓗ One 8mm sterling silver hollow round

Ⓘ One 10mm sterling silver hollow patterned square

Ⓙ Four 6mm Swarovski crystal bicones

Ⓚ Three 45–50mm woven beads, two of crystal AB and one of jet, each comprising thirty 4mm bicones, (see instructions below)

Agate, jasper, howlite, and lava stone

Sherril Olive ~ Dusk to Dawn

This is a striking monochromatic necklace that is almost sculptural in design. The piece features white agate, zebra jasper, bamboo jasper, howlite, and two lovely lava stone rectangular beads, with beautiful sparkling globes nestling in their hollows, made by weaving 4mm Swarovski crystals into shape. The silver accent beads and clasp complete the piece perfectly.

You will also need:
● Stringing material
● Sterling silver 25mm heart toggle clasp
● Two 2x2mm sterling silver crimp beads
● Two 3mm sterling silver crimp covers

Make woven beads first, then start stringing the necklace here.

Adjust length from either side of clasp as required.

Ⓚ Woven beads
Cut 51cm (20in.) of 0.35mm cord (Fireline or monofilament). Pair the ends so you have a "right" thread (shown in blue) and a "left" thread (shown in red). String the beads in the numbered order using the right and left threads as shown in the diagram (left).

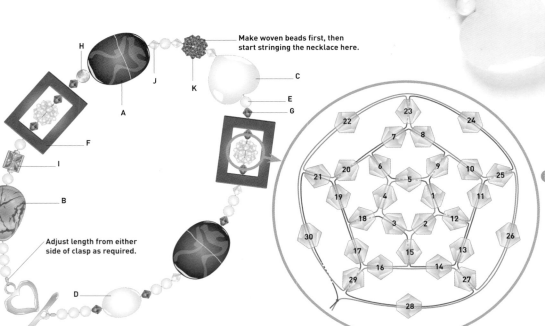

Turquoise and onyx

Christelle Greaves ~ Inca Treasure

Vibrant turquoise with gorgeous veining, and dark, mysterious onyx form the focal point of this amazing neckpiece. This elegant and flattering long-line necklace, with intricate detailing in the chain section, is perfectly balanced and in classical colours that simply won't date.

● Approximate length 56cm (22in.)

BEAD STORE

Ⓐ One 30mm black onyx disc

Ⓑ Two 12x8mm turquoise rondelles

Ⓒ 3g of size 5 black seed beads

Ⓓ 1g of size 6 turquoise seed beads

Ⓔ 1g of size 8 turquoise seed beads

Ⓕ Twenty-seven 4mm Swarovski AB crystals

You will also need:

● Stringing material
● Silver-plated 10mm trigger clasp
● Four 2x2mm sterling silver crimp beads
● Four 3mm sterling silver crimp covers
● Approximately 15cm (6in.) of silver-plated chain cut into smaller lengths as appropriate
● Four sterling silver head pins
● Two 6mm silver-plated split rings, one to attach the chain and dangles to stringing material, and one to fasten

Create the dangles first and attach to split ring. Loop stringing material through onyx focal and attach to split ring. String remaining beads from above focal.

Amazonite and rose quartz

Trudi Doherty ~ Spring Leaf

The lush green of the amazonite leaves and the blossom-like softness of the rose quartz give this beautiful necklace a springtime feel. The artist has achieved a good sense of balance both within the colour scheme and the layout of the necklace. Adding a few silver accent beads shows off the gemstones in all of their natural beauty.

F

Start here

C

E

D

B

G

A

- Approximate length 50cm (19¾in.), not including central drop

BEAD STORE

- (A) Three 40mm amazonite carved leaves
- (B) Eighteen 8mm faceted amazonite buttons
- (C) Fifty-eight 5–6mm rose quartz rounds
- (D) Four 8mm rose quartz rounds
- (E) Thirty-one 4mm Bali silver daisy spacers
- (F) Fifteen 4mm Swarovski volcano bicones
- (G) Three 3mm Swarovski volcano bicones

You will also need:

- Beading wire
- Silver toggle clasp
- Two 2x2mm sterling silver crimp beads
- Two 3mm sterling silver crimp covers

Amazonite

Heather Marrow ~ Kiss of the Valkyrie

This is a stunningly beautiful two-strand necklace that uses amazing icy blue amazonite briolettes as the focal point on the outer strand and an abundance of rounds on both strands, creating a very substantial piece. The design on the silver beads is intricate yet not overpowering, and the introduction of jet and ruby beads adds warmth, making this a truly opulent design.

● Approximate length: inner strand 44.5cm (17½in.); outer strand 48cm (19in.) with a 2.5cm (1in.) extension

BEAD STORE

A Three 18x25mm amazonite briolettes

B Seventy-six 6mm amazonite rounds

C Twenty-seven 4x6mm faceted jet rondelles

D Seventy-six 10/0 ruby lustre rocaille seed beads

E Two approximately 25mm silver-plated cones

F Seven 8mm sterling silver shell spacers

G Fourteen 8mm sterling silver knot spacers

You will also need:

● Two 61-cm (24-in.) lengths of 7-strand Beadalon wire

● Three 10-cm (4-in.) lengths of 0.8mm (20-gauge) sterling silver wire, one at each cone end and one to make a toggle bar

● Four 2x2mm sterling silver crimp beads

● 7.5cm (3in.) silver-plated eye pin

● Twelve 4mm (⅛in.) 0.8mm (20-gauge) sterling silver jump rings

● Three 12mm (½in.) 1.3mm (16-gauge) sterling silver jump rings

Make a coiled loop at one end of the sterling silver wire. Feed the ends of both strands of Beadalon through the loop, back over, and through a few beads, then secure with a crimp bead. Feed the long end of wire remaining through the cone and coil loop to secure.

Start from the centre of each strand.

A

B

C

D

E

F

G

Sodalite

Christelle Greaves ~ Tempest

The sodalite used in this piece has soft mottling and is a rich blue, almost the colour of a stormy sky. The artist has incorporated a pleasing variety of bead shapes and the free-form wrapping and zigzag dangles are contemporary in style. This is a versatile and desirable item of jewellery.

- Approximate length 49cm (19in.)

BEAD STORE

- **A** One approximately 60mm long sodalite stone, undrilled
- **B** Four 25mm sodalite rectangles
- **C** 3g of size 11 blue/grey seed beads
- **D** Four 8mm silver-plated textured beads
- **E** Eighteen 4mm silver-plated round spacers
- **F** Two 10mm Swarovski slider beads
- **G** Fourteen 4mm Swarovski dark blue bicones
- **H** One Tibetan silver hanger bead

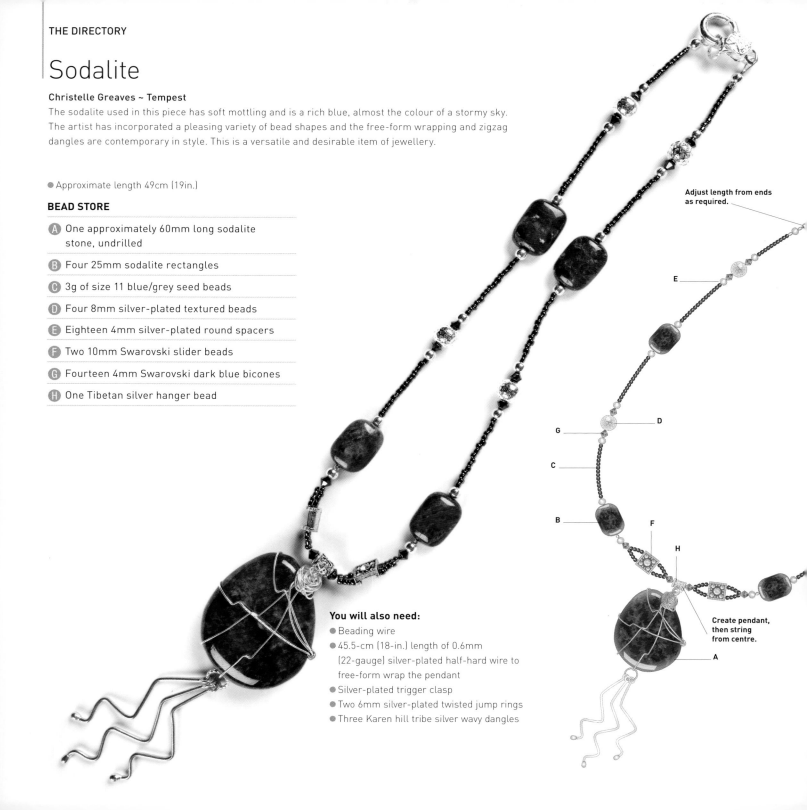

Adjust length from ends as required.

Create pendant, then string from centre.

You will also need:
- Beading wire
- 45.5-cm (18-in.) length of 0.6mm (22-gauge) silver-plated half-hard wire to free-form wrap the pendant
- Silver-plated trigger clasp
- Two 6mm silver-plated twisted jump rings
- Three Karen hill tribe silver wavy dangles

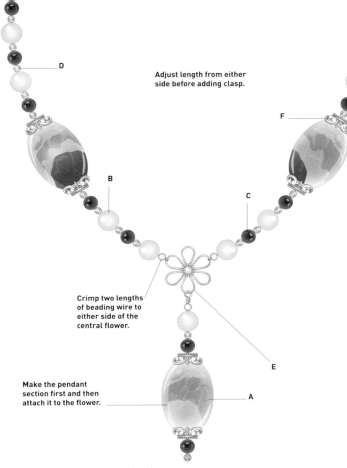

Adjust length from either side before adding clasp.

Crimp two lengths of beading wire to either side of the central flower.

Make the pendant section first and then attach it to the flower.

Amazonite and blackstone

Kim Gover ~ Amazon

The amazonite ovals featured here have an interesting bloom across them and a strong variation in colour, which makes it possible to set them in the alternating pattern of the neckpiece. The "Y" style sits well against the body and can be carried from day to evening wear.

- Approximate length 48cm (19in.)

BEAD STORE

Ⓐ Three 30x20mm amazonite ovals

Ⓑ Twenty-one 8mm amazonite rounds

Ⓒ Twenty-one 6mm blackstone rounds

Ⓓ Forty-two 3mm Karen hill tribe silver spacers

Ⓔ One sterling silver flower connector

Ⓕ Six scrolled lentil bead caps

You will also need:

- Beading wire
- Silver "S" clasp
- Four 2x2mm sterling silver crimp beads
- Four 3mm sterling silver crimp covers
- One 50mm sterling silver head pin

Watermelon tourmaline

Jennifer Airs ~ Tourmaline Temptation

This necklace is a delicate creation that features gorgeously juicy watermelon tourmaline briolettes: the play of colour in these is beautiful and you can see exactly why the stone has been named. The style is simple and showcases the tourmaline to perfection, creating a necklace that will certainly turn heads.

D

Start here

B

C

A

● Approximate length 43cm (17in.)

BEAD STORE

Ⓐ Seven watermelon tourmaline briolettes, graduated from 5mm to 10mm

Ⓑ Twenty 3mm Swarovski crystal AB bicones

Ⓒ Ten 4mm Swarovski crystal AB bicones

Ⓓ 1g of size 15 silver-plated seed beads

You will also need:

● 51-cm (20-in.) length of Soft Flex beading wire
● Karen hill tribe silver toggle clasp
● Two 2x2mm sterling silver crimp beads
● Two sterling silver wire guardians

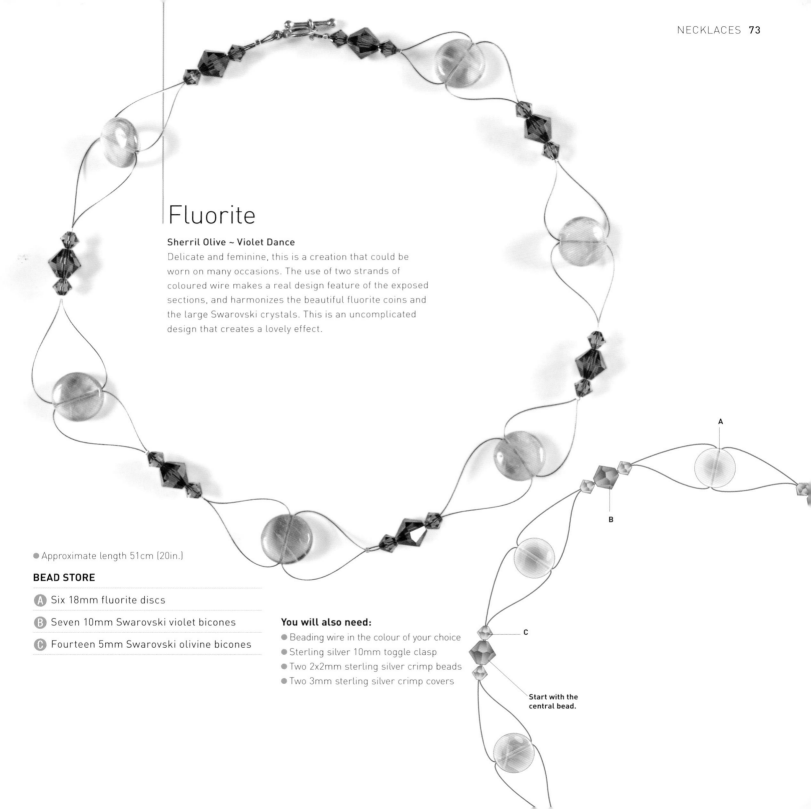

Fluorite

Sherril Olive ~ Violet Dance

Delicate and feminine, this is a creation that could be
worn on many occasions. The use of two strands of
coloured wire makes a real design feature of the exposed
sections, and harmonizes the beautiful fluorite coins and
the large Swarovski crystals. This is an uncomplicated
design that creates a lovely effect.

● Approximate length 51cm (20in.)

BEAD STORE

A Six 18mm fluorite discs

B Seven 10mm Swarovski violet bicones

C Fourteen 5mm Swarovski olivine bicones

You will also need:
● Beading wire in the colour of your choice
● Sterling silver 10mm toggle clasp
● Two 2x2mm sterling silver crimp beads
● Two 3mm sterling silver crimp covers

A

B

C

Start with the
central bead.

Lava stone and opal

Sherril Olive ~ Volcano

Striking colours make a real statement in this piece. The lava stone beads are fascinating in texture, and the fire opal faceted Swarovski crystals are reminiscent of the hot flowing lava that created them. The design is easy to wear and the pendant focal section will draw the eye and elongate the neckline.

Create pendant section first, then string from the centre.

A

B

C

- Approximate length 39cm (15½in.)

BEAD STORE

A Thirty-one 12x8mm lava stone rondelles

B Seventeen 8mm Swarovski fire opal rounds

C Two 2.5–4cm (1–1½in.) gold-plated leaves

You will also need:
- Beading wire
- 9ct gold 20mm figure-of-eight clasp
- Four 2x2mm 9ct gold crimp beads
- One 7.5-cm (3-in.) length of gold-plated chain
- Two gold-plated jump rings to attach the leaves to the chain
- Gold-plated head pin

- Approximate length 47cm (18½in.)

BEAD STORE

Ⓐ Eight 25x18mm Botswana agate ovals

Ⓑ 5g of size 11 satin gold Miyuki Delica seed beads

Ⓒ Three 10mm Swarovski light Colorado topaz rounds

Ⓓ Sixteen 4mm Swarovski padparadscha bicones

Ⓔ Eighteen 4mm gold-plated cubes

Ⓕ Three 6mm Swarovski starshine opal vintage bicones

Ⓖ Four 6mm Swarovski smoky quartz bicones

You will also need:
- Stringing material
- 9ct gold 18mm trigger and 9ct gold 8mm ring for the clasp
- Two 2x2mm 9ct gold crimp beads

Botswana agate

Sherril Olive ~ Grand Canyon

This necklace contains beautiful slices of Botswana agate, which show the many patterns and colourways that the stone can manifest. The artist has enhanced these with Swarovski crystals in warm browns and golden tones with a hint of deep orange. The overall effect is earthy, organic, and rich, making this a very desirable piece of jewellery.

Start here

A   B   C   D   E   F   G

Quartz and serpentine

Sherril Olive ~ Spring

For this substantial and eye-catching necklace the artist has used an interesting asymmetric stringing style on all of the strands, and the choice of irregularly shaped stones enhances this. The petrol blue quartz is the perfect foil for the vibrant serpentine.

● Approximate length 52cm (20½in.)

BEAD STORE

Ⓐ Fifty-five 12mm petrol blue quartz squared ovals

Ⓑ Twenty-two 24–30mm frosted serpentine irregular ovals

Ⓒ 2g of size 11 petrol blue Miyuki Delica seed beads

Ⓓ 5g of size 8 frosted lime green seed beads

You will also need:
● Stringing material
● Sterling silver hook-and-ring clasp
● Two three-bar sterling silver necklace ends
● Six 2x2mm sterling silver crimp beads
● Six 3mm sterling silver crimp covers

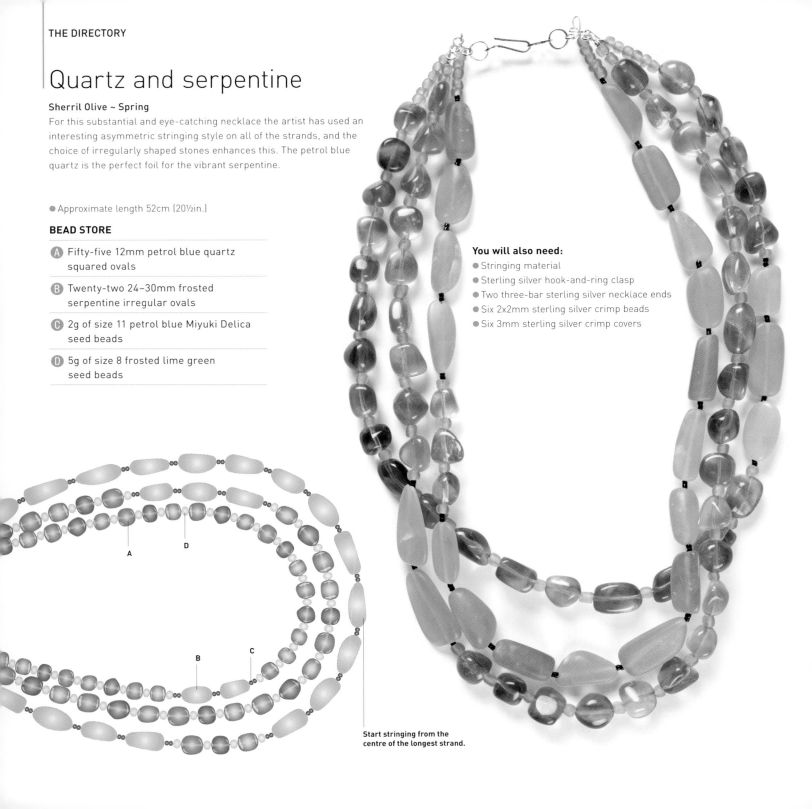

Start stringing from the centre of the longest strand.

Amazonite and aventurine

Sherril Olive ~ Sea Foam

This gorgeous necklace contains myriad colours reminiscent of a deep green ocean. The faceted amazonite stones have lovely, softly toned markings and reflect the light just like the sun hitting a cresting wave. The artist has teamed these with aventurine rondelles and Swarovski crystals, which add depth and balance.

● Approximate length 52cm (20½in.)

BEAD STORE

(A) Thirteen 12x18mm faceted amazonite ovals

(B) Eleven 12mm aventurine rondelles

(C) Ten 6mm Swarovski Pacific opal rounds

(D) Ten 4mm Swarovski Pacific opal bicones

(E) Seven 6mm Swarovski Montana bicones

(F) Six 6mm Swarovski light azore bicones

(G) 2g of size 11 matte black Miyuki Delica seed beads

(H) Twenty-five 3–4mm sterling silver daisy spacers

You will also need:
● Stringing material
● Sterling silver toggle clasp
● Two 2x2mm sterling silver crimp beads
● Two 3mm sterling silver crimp covers

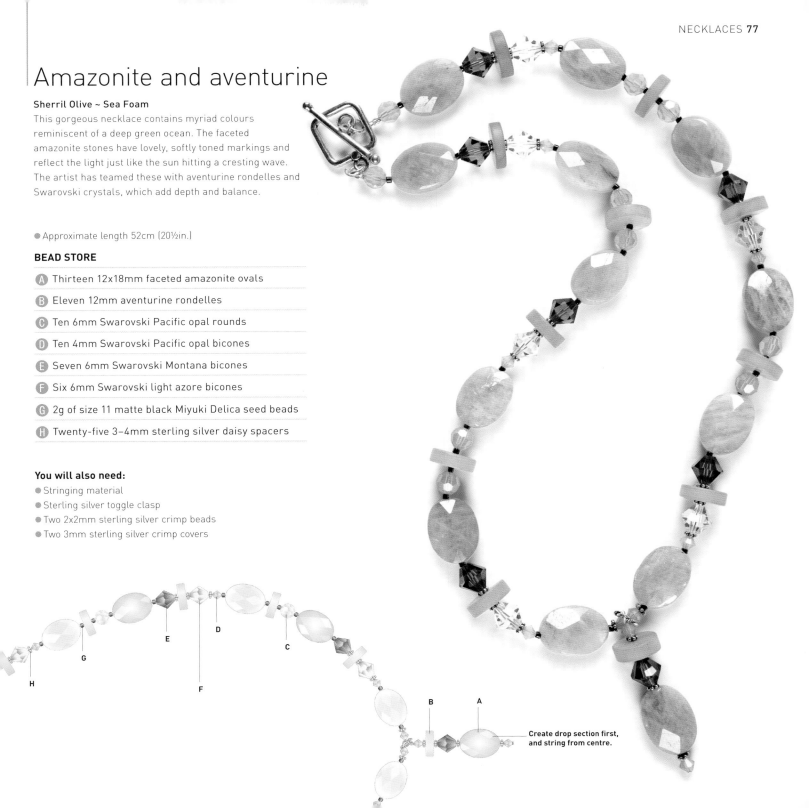

Create drop section first, and string from centre.

Turquoise

Maria Joao Rebelo ~ Trio

This necklace is contemporary in style, with the large turquoise focal designed to sit at the base of the throat while the remaining length of the necklace is wrapped around as a second strand, with the clasp sitting below the focal. The artist has carefully selected two lampworked beads to harmonize the colours in the whole piece, and the addition of the well spaced silver rondelles adds brightness and lift.

● Approximate length 90cm (35½in.)

BEAD STORE

Ⓐ One 39.5-cm (15½-in.) string of turquoise chips

Ⓑ One 40mm turquoise oval

Ⓒ Two 30mm lampworked ovals

Ⓓ Four 13mm Czech black glass rondelles

Ⓔ Ten 10mm Czech black glass rounds

Ⓕ Four 4x3mm Czech black glass rondelles

Ⓖ Thirty 5mm sterling silver rondelles

Ⓗ Thirty-four 2mm sterling silver rounds

Ⓘ Two 4mm sterling silver stacked beads

You will also need:
● Stringing material
● One 25mm (1in.) silver "S" clasp
● Two 2x2mm sterling silver crimp beads

A

B

Start here

C

D

E

F

G

H

I

Adjust length from either side of clasp as required.

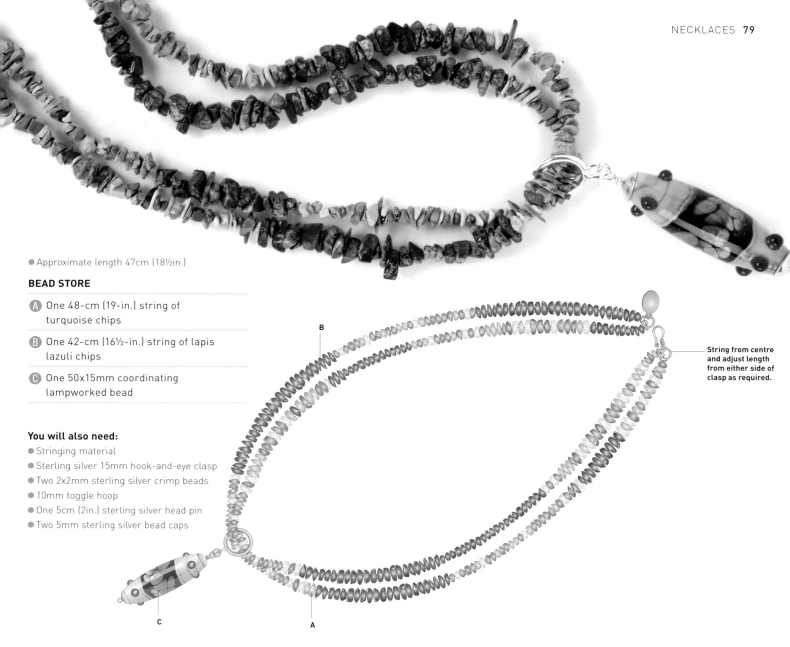

● Approximate length 47cm (18½in.)

BEAD STORE

Ⓐ One 48-cm (19-in.) string of turquoise chips

Ⓑ One 42-cm (16½-in.) string of lapis lazuli chips

Ⓒ One 50x15mm coordinating lampworked bead

You will also need:
● Stringing material
● Sterling silver 15mm hook-and-eye clasp
● Two 2x2mm sterling silver crimp beads
● 10mm toggle hoop
● One 5cm (2in.) sterling silver head pin
● Two 5mm sterling silver bead caps

B

A

String from centre and adjust length from either side of clasp as required.

C

Turquoise and lapis lazuli

Maria Joao Rebelo ~ Belong Together
This necklace demonstrates a very effective way of using chips for an arresting design. The rich green of the turquoise and the dark blue lapis have been unified in the focal lampworked bead. The artist has made innovative use of a toggle hoop here to slide over both strands of chips at once.

Bracelets

Jade and jasper

Lisa Taylor ~ Dreamcatcher

This southwest-style bracelet utilizes candy jade, red jasper, and a variety of patterned ethnic beads to achieve an especially attractive result. The detailed silver feather charms balance the piece and give it individuality.

● Approximate length 19cm (7½in.)

BEAD STORE

Ⓐ Five 7mm blue candy jade rounds

Ⓑ Eleven 4mm red jasper rounds

Ⓒ Two 8mm cane glass beads

Ⓓ One 20mm silver focal bead

Ⓔ Two 12mm silver diamond beads

Ⓕ Four 9mm silver lotus flower spacers

Ⓖ Four 4mm patterned spacers

Ⓗ Four 5mm disc spacers

Ⓘ Two large silver feather charms

Start here

D

C

F

B

E

H

G

A

Adjust size from either side of clasp as required.

I

You will also need:
● Stringing material
● Sterling silver toggle clasp
● Two 2x2mm sterling silver crimp beads
● Two 3mm sterling silver crimp covers
● Sterling silver head pin
● Sterling silver jump ring

Blue opal

Karin Chilton ~ Blue Moon

This bracelet portrays the natural, organic quality of the blue opal nuggets with beautiful simplicity. The hammered silver focal disc brings light to the piece without detracting from the gemstones, and the pearls are an inspired choice for accent beads.

● Approximate length 19cm (7½in.)

BEAD STORE

Ⓐ Six 10x8mm blue opal nuggets

Ⓑ Four 5mm freshwater rice pearls

Ⓒ One 22mm Karen hill tribe silver hammered disc

Ⓓ Two 7mm Karen hill tribe silver coiled beads

Ⓔ Eight 4mm Bali sterling silver daisy spacers

Ⓕ Two 4mm Swarovski Pacific opal bicones

You will also need:
● Stringing material ● Silver toggle clasp ● Two calottes
● Sterling silver split ring ● Silver shell charm

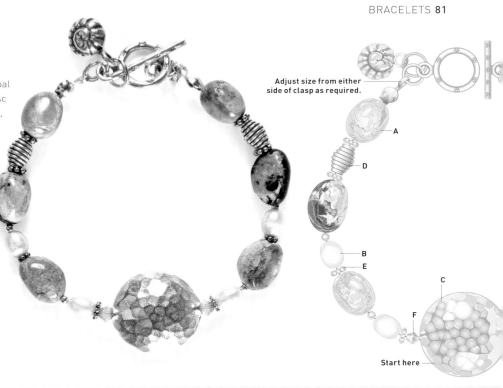

Adjust size from either side of clasp as required.

Start here

Dumortierite and blue goldstone

● Approximate length 17cm (6¾in.)

BEAD STORE

Ⓐ Three 20mm dumortierite coins (offset drilled)

Ⓑ Ten 8mm blue goldstone rounds

Ⓒ Four 6mm Bali silver patterned beads

Ⓓ Eight 3mm Karen hill tribe silver spacers

Kim Gover ~ Midnight Sparkle
Three deep blue dumortierite discs overlap to form the unusual focal point of this bracelet, enhanced with subtly sparkling blue goldstone rounds and lifted with ornate Bali silver spacer beads. This is an easy-to-wear piece to take you from day wear straight into evening.

You will also need:
● Stringing material
● Silver toggle clasp
● Two 2x2mm sterling silver crimp beads
● Two 3mm sterling silver crimp covers

Adjust size from either side of clasp as required.

Start here

Malachite

Diane Fairhall ~ Genevieve

A stunning and versatile timepiece, this watch
can be worn equally well with evening wear
or a more casual style of clothing. The vividly
coloured malachite beads implemented here have
wonderful striations, and the artist has teamed
them perfectly with copper and silver beads
and toggle.

● Approximate length 19cm (7½in.)

BEAD STORE

Ⓐ Eight 10mm malachite coins

Ⓑ Four 8x4mm copper tubes

Ⓒ Two 12x9mm copper/silver rondelles

Start here

A

B   C

Adjust length
from either
side of clasp
as required.

You will also need:

● Watch face
● Stringing material
● Copper/silver toggle clasp
● Four 2x2mm crimp beads
● Four 3mm copper crimp covers

Malachite and silver

Anita Seeberg ~ Spring

This eye-catching piece has been created using stunning malachite beads containing wonderful
striations of darker green throughout. An abundance of Thai silver components in many
different shapes enhances the bold colour of the malachite and makes this a substantial,
unique, and highly desirable bracelet.

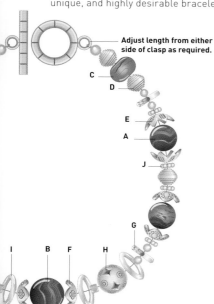

Adjust length from either
side of clasp as required.

C
D
E
A
J
G
I B F H

Start here

● Approximate length 20cm (8in.)

BEAD STORE

Ⓐ Four 9mm malachite rounds

Ⓑ One 11mm malachite round

Ⓒ Two 10mm green
lampworked spacers

Ⓓ Six 6mm Karen hill tribe
silver coiled beads

Ⓔ Eight 9mm Karen hill tribe
silver design bead caps

Ⓕ Two 11mm Karen hill tribe silver
design bead caps

Ⓖ Four 8mm Karen hill tribe silver washer
spacer beads

Ⓗ Two 10mm Karen hill tribe silver design
round beads

Ⓘ Four 10mm Karen hill tribe silver
hammered flat jump rings

Ⓙ Eight 4mm sterling silver daisy spacers

You will also need:

● Stringing material
● Silver toggle clasp
● Two 2x2mm sterling silver crimp beads
● Two 4mm sterling silver crimp covers

You will also need:
- Stringing material
- Sterling silver lobster clasp
- Four 2x2mm sterling silver crimp beads
- Two wire guardians

Ruby in zoisite

Karin Chilton ~ Vert et Rouge

The three ruby in zoisite rectangular beads subsume some wonderful colour variations, and the artist has offset these perfectly with small emerald beads and ruby-coloured crystals. The hexagonal silver beads maintain the proportions of the bracelet very well, and the combination of the geometric shapes is aesthetically pleasing.

- Approximate length 21cm (8¼in.)

BEAD STORE

A Three 18mm ruby in zoisite rectangles

B Two 12mm Karen hill tribe silver hexagonal beads

C Six 3–4mm emerald rondelles

D Six 6mm Swarovski ruby bicones

E Four 4mm Karen hill tribe silver coiled beads

F Ten 2mm sterling silver round beads

G Six 6mm sterling silver bead caps

H Eight 4mm Bali silver daisy spacers

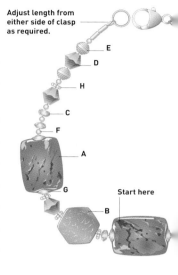

Adjust length from either side of clasp as required.

Start here

Tourmaline

Colette Ladley ~ Muted Rainbow

This fabulous and funky bracelet in an easy-to-wear style really shows off the amazing array of colours that tourmaline can manifest. A simple design using chips and faceted rounds allows this lovely gemstone to speak for itself.

- Approximate length 20cm (8in.)

BEAD STORE

A Six 8mm faceted tourmaline rounds

B Approximately forty-five tourmaline chips

C Six small copper head pins

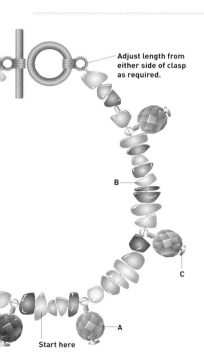

Adjust length from either side of clasp as required.

B

C

A

Start here

You will also need:
- Stringing material
- Toggle clasp
- Two 2x2mm copper crimp beads

Amethyst and peridot

Carol Mogg ~ Papillon

Simple in style but still very elegant, this lovely bracelet features rich faceted amethyst beads, teamed with contrasting peridot stones to great effect. The beautiful silver butterfly toggle clasp is a real design feature and sets off the piece perfectly.

● Approximate length 19cm (7½in.)

BEAD STORE

Ⓐ Fifteen 6mm faceted amethyst rounds

Ⓑ Fourteen 2–3mm faceted peridot rounds

Ⓒ Four 4mm peridot rounds

Ⓓ Thai silver leaf charm

You will also need:
● Stringing material
● Bali silver toggle clasp
● Two crimp tubes or two clamshell calottes
● Dab of hypo-epoxy cement to secure knots

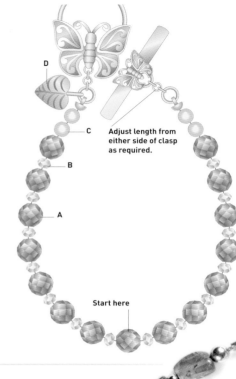

Adjust length from either side of clasp as required.

Start here

Iolite

Trudi Doherty ~ Violet Dream

This stylish bracelet has been created using pretty iolite rectangles that contain some interesting markings and have a delicate colour, wonderfully enhanced by the focal lampworked bead. Crystals and Bali silver brighten the design for classic wearability.

● Approximate length 19.5cm (7¾in.)

BEAD STORE

Ⓐ Fifteen 5mm iolite rectangles

Ⓑ One lampworked focal

Ⓒ Two bead caps suitable for focal

Ⓓ Five 4mm Swarovski tanzanite cubes

Ⓔ Three 6mm Swarovski titan bicones

Ⓕ Seven 4mm Bali silver daisy spacers

Ⓖ Fourteen 2mm sterling silver round beads

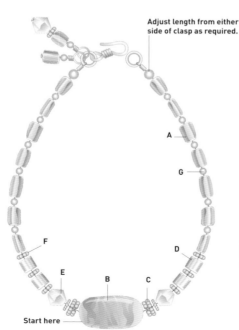

Adjust length from either side of clasp as required.

Start here

You will also need:
● Beading wire
● Hook-and-eye clasp
● Two 2x2mm sterling silver crimp beads
● Two sterling silver head pins

Fluorite

Kim Gover ~ Ethereal

This softly toned, charming bracelet features fluorite coin beads that display wonderful shades of lilac and green, which are accented by the delicate crystal dangles that adorn the circumference and catch the light. Floral-patterned Karen hill tribe silver beads add structure and lift, and the ornate toggle fastening completes this feminine piece.

● Approximate length 19.5cm (7¾in.)

BEAD STORE

Ⓐ Six 12mm fluorite coins

Ⓑ Five 8x6mm Karen hill tribe silver floral beads

Ⓒ Twelve 5mm sterling silver jump rings

Ⓓ Twelve sterling silver head pins

Ⓔ Thirty-six sterling silver eye pins

Ⓕ Twelve 6mm Swarovski light emerald bicones

Ⓖ Twenty-four 4mm Swarovski light amethyst bicones

Ⓗ Twenty-four 4mm Swarovski erinite bicones

You will also need:

● Stringing material
● Silver toggle clasp
● Two 2x2mm sterling silver crimp beads
● Two 3mm sterling silver crimp covers

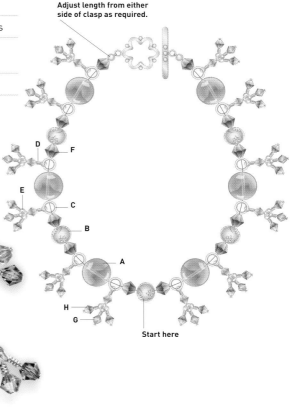

Adjust length from either side of clasp as required.

D   F
E   C
B
A
H
G

Start here

Rose quartz

Vicki Honeywill ~ Candy Floss

A gorgeous abundance of rose quartz features in this wonderfully feminine bracelet. The focal nugget and the two round stones show the richness of colour that rose quartz can achieve, while the clusters of chips in this clever design are soft and delicate in colour, and add weight and harmony to the piece.

Start here. Take one 6-cm (2½-in.) length of sterling silver wire and make a wrapped loop at one end. Crimp the three strands of tiger tail to this. Insert the straight end of the wire into the widest part of the cone and make a new wrapped loop at the narrow end to attach the toggle to.

I

D

C

H

Adjust bracelet size by reducing length of chip sections.

E

F

B

G

A

You will also need:

- Silver toggle clasp
- Three 25-cm (10-in.) lengths of tiger tail or similar
- Two 6-cm (2½-in.) lengths of 0.6mm (22-gauge) sterling silver wire
- Six 2x2mm sterling silver crimp beads
- Two sterling silver head pins
- Rose charm

- Approximate length 20cm (8in.)

BEAD STORE

A	One 20mm rose quartz nugget
B	Two 12mm rose quartz rounds
C	Two 4mm rose quartz rounds
D	One 6mm rose quartz round
E	Approximately one hundred rose quartz chips
F	Eighteen 4mm sterling silver round beads
G	Six 10mm Bali silver bead caps
H	Two 10x14mm Bali silver cones
I	One 6mm Bali silver bead cap

Blue lace agate and clear quartz

Kim Gover ~ Cinderella

A shimmering array of soft pastel stones and sparkling crystals features in this romantically designed watch. The delicately banded blue lace agate brings colour, while the clear quartz chips and crystals add sparkle. The glass pearls lend weight and harmonize the three strands, which are designed to be twisted before fastening.

● Approximate length 20cm (8in.)

BEAD STORE

Ⓐ Twelve 8mm blue lace agate rounds

Ⓑ Twenty-two clear quartz chips

Ⓒ Thirteen 6mm ivory glass pearls

Ⓓ Five 6mm filigree metal rounds

Ⓔ Sixteen 4mm Swarovski clear AB bicones

Ⓕ Sixteen 3mm metal round spacers

Ⓖ Two 6mm basket bead caps

Ⓗ Two 6mm flat filigree bead caps

Ⓘ Three 6mm twisted jump rings

Ⓙ Swarovski butterfly bead

Ⓚ Tibetan silver butterfly bead

You will also need:

● Watch face ● Three 30.5-cm (12-in.) lengths of Acculon or similar ● Silver toggle clasp ● Two 2x2mm sterling silver crimp beads ● Two 3mm sterling silver crimp covers ● Two sterling silver head pins

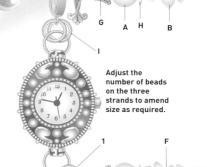

Start here

G A H B

Adjust the number of beads on the three strands to amend size as required.

1 F

I

J C E

K D

Start from the main loop of the toggle and work across to point 1. From here string the three strands and crimp with one crimp bead. String the first bead cap, bead, and second bead cap over all three wires, then string each wire individually.

Pearl

Kanina Wolff ~ Moonlight Rendezvous

An elegant watch made with beautiful and ever-popular pearls. This watch has a classic style with a modern twist in the form of the wire-wrapped sections, echoed in the scrollwork on the watch face. The large pearls balance the size of the watch face and the delicate dangle finishes the piece perfectly.

● Approximate length 20cm (8in.)

BEAD STORE

Ⓐ Eight 10mm freshwater ivory pearl semi-coins

Ⓑ Seven 4mm Swarovski cream roe glass pearls

Ⓒ 38cm (15in.) of 0.5mm (24-gauge) sterling silver wire

Ⓓ Three sterling silver head pins

You will also need:

● Watch face
● Silver toggle clasp

Add or remove wrapped sections to adjust length as required.

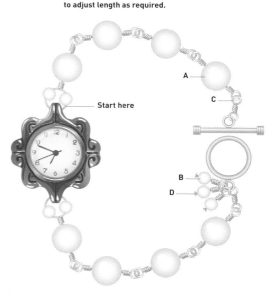

Start here

A

C

B

D

Sponge coral

Phillipa Wilson ~ The Art of Nature

To form this design the artist has chosen excellent sponge coral beads that are vivid in colour with a swirling, natural yellow pattern. There is a fascinating mixture of textures in this piece that draws the eye in. The sponge coral looks amazingly tactile with its raised matte finish, and the contrast with the smooth, shiny surface of the silver-plated ceramic cubes provides a great visual effect.

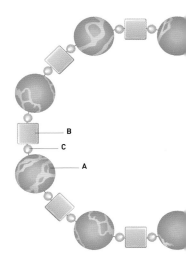

- Approximate length 20cm (8in.)

You will also need:
- Stretch stringing material
- A dab of hypo-epoxy cement to secure knot

BEAD STORE

- Ⓐ Eight 13mm sponge coral rounds
- Ⓑ Eight 6mm sterling-silver coated ceramic cubes
- Ⓒ Sixteen 2mm sterling silver rounds

- Approximate length 22cm (8½in.)

BEAD STORE

- Ⓐ Four 8mm carnelian rounds
- Ⓑ Two 8mm faceted black glass rounds
- Ⓒ Six 4mm faceted black glass rounds
- Ⓓ Three animal-print lampworked beads
- Ⓔ Twelve 4mm black jump rings

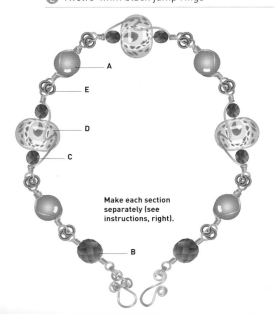

Make each section separately (see instructions, right).

Carnelian

Nan Fry ~ Animal Instinct

In this striking bracelet the carnelian is used as the perfect foil for the lampworked beads. The animal-print lampworked contains some lovely warm colours and great patterns, and the carnelian adds spice and zing to the whole piece. The copper wirework enhances the decorative effect of the finished piece.

You will also need:
- Hook-and-eye clasp
- Nine 20-cm (8-in.) lengths of 0.6mm (22-gauge) copper wire

This bracelet is made in sections, then connected with jump rings.

1. Cut about 20cm (8in.) of wire and make a wrapped loop at one end. Thread on the bead or beads, depending on which loop you are making.

2. Make a second wrapped loop at the other end. Do not cut off the long piece of wire you should have left. Take this long length of wire and trail it around the bead to the other end (the first wrapped loop), hook it around and trail it back down again. Wrap the wire around the second wrapped loop until it is secure and neat, then cut off the remainder.

3. For the larger links with animal print beads in, make a kink in the wire with flat-nosed pliers. Only trail the wire one way. The trick is not to make the wire very tight when you trail it around the bead, then it will kink nicely to take up the slack.

Carnelian, garnet, and peridot

Vicki Honeywill ~ Autumn Blossom

Gorgeous carved carnelian flowers form the focal point of this bracelet. Peridot and garnet accent beads provide a rich autumn colour scheme, and have been teamed with Thai silver tubes for a stylish, easy-to-wear design.

- Approximate length 18cm (7in.)

BEAD STORE

- **A** One 22mm carnelian flower
- **B** Two 12mm carnelian flowers
- **C** Seven 5mm peridot rounds
- **D** One 6mm peridot oval
- **E** Eleven 4mm garnet rounds
- **F** One 8mm garnet oval
- **G** Seven 4mm sterling silver daisy spacers
- **H** Two 30mm Thai silver curved tubes

You will also need:
- Stringing material
- Silver toggle clasp
- Two 2x2mm crimp beads
- Two 4mm sterling silver crimp covers
- Two sterling silver head pins

Adjust length from either side of clasp as required.

Start here

Kambaba jasper and limestone

Gaile Almrott ~ Galactic Storm

The artist has used a focal bead of fascinating kambaba jasper and an abundance of limestone to create this arresting bracelet. The focal disc clearly shows the distinctive markings and swirling patterns that lend the stone its other name "star galaxy jasper". Subtle accents of silver integrate perfectly.

- Approximate length 19.5cm (7¾in.)

BEAD STORE

- **A** One 20mm kambaba jasper disc
- **B** Twenty 6mm limestone heishi beads
- **C** Two 6mm Swarovski jet rounds
- **D** Ten 4mm Swarovski morion bicones
- **E** Two sterling silver lentil bead caps
- **F** Four 4mm sterling silver bead caps
- **G** Two 6mm Karen hill tribe silver beads
- **H** Eight 6mm Karen hill tribe silver discs
- **I** Sixteen 3mm Karen hill tribe silver bicones

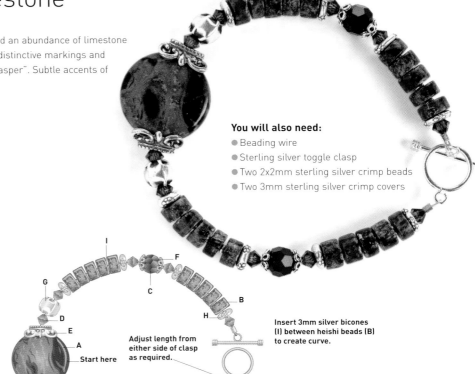

You will also need:
- Beading wire
- Sterling silver toggle clasp
- Two 2x2mm sterling silver crimp beads
- Two 3mm sterling silver crimp covers

Insert 3mm silver bicones (I) between heishi beads (B) to create curve.

Adjust length from either side of clasp as required.

Start here

Unakite and amber

Terry West ~ Jupiter

This amazing charm bracelet is absolutely loaded with unakite and amber dangles. The amber is a rich colour with some fascinating inclusions, and the unakite has its characteristic mottled green and pink markings. The pairing of these stones is quite unusual but very effective. The gold chain complements the colours of the gemstones, and the extra charm at the clasp helps to weight the piece correctly.

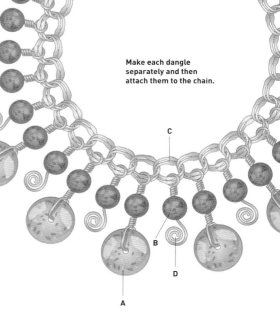

Make each dangle separately and then attach them to the chain.

- Approximate length adjustable from 18 to 20cm (7 to 8in.)

BEAD STORE

(A) Thirteen 10mm amber pressed disc beads

(B) Twenty-five 7mm unakite rounds

(C) One 16.5-cm (6½-in.) length of double ring gold-filled chain

(D) One approximately 127-cm (50-in.) length of gold-filled wire (allows 5cm [2in.] per charm)

You will also need:

- Gold-filled lobster clasp
- 4-cm (1½-in.) length of small gold-filled chain for extender

Pink rhodonite and smoky quartz

Kim Booth ~ In Bloom

Vibrant pink rhodonite coins give visual impact here, while the addition of the smoky quartz faceted rondelles provides a subtle yet perfect foil for the large beads. The unusual floral bead caps give character and add lift to the bracelet, while the toggle clasp brings harmony by echoing both the shape of the coins and the patterning on the bead caps.

- Approximate length 20cm (8in.)

BEAD STORE

- Ⓐ Five 20mm rhodonite coins
- Ⓑ Ten 6mm Bali silver folded bead caps
- Ⓒ Six 6mm faceted smoky quartz rondelles
- Ⓓ Twelve 4mm sterling silver rounds

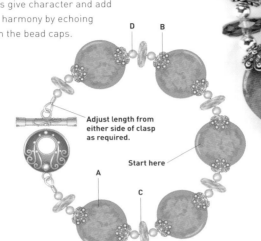

Adjust length from either side of clasp as required.

Start here

You will also need:

- 25-cm (10-in.) length of Soft Touch beading wire
- Bali silver toggle clasp
- Two 2x2mm sterling silver crimp beads
- Two large sterling silver wire guardians

Rhyolite

Jennifer Airs ~ Rhyolite Reward

Rhyolite, with its extraordinary marbled markings, is the focus for this pretty bracelet. The artist has teamed the ovals with some coordinating lampworked beads and has created an ornate spiral clasp by free-form wire wrapping. The secondary seed bead strand winding around the length of the bracelet finishes off the piece to perfection.

- Approximate length 16cm (6¼in.)

BEAD STORE

- Ⓐ Five 18x12mm rhyolite ovals
- Ⓑ Two 12mm lampworked beads
- Ⓒ 1g of size 8 Miyuki seed beads

You will also need:

- One 40-cm (16-in.) length of gold-coloured beading wire
- One 51-cm (20-in.) length of gold-plated 0.5mm (24-gauge) wire for clasp
- Two 9ct gold crimp beads

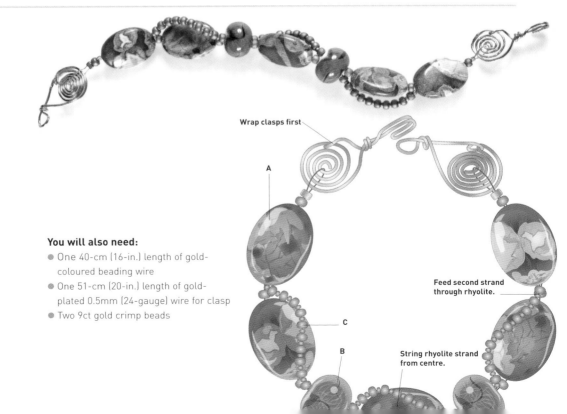

Wrap clasps first

Feed second strand through rhyolite.

String rhyolite strand from centre.

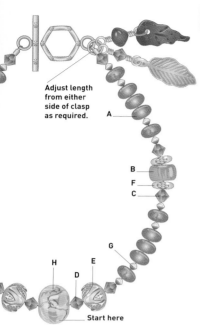

Adjust length from either side of clasp as required.

A

B
F
C

G

H   E
  D

Start here

Turquoise and coral

Gaile Almrott ~ Southwest Trail

This bracelet instantly provokes thoughts of Native American jewellery, with gorgeous veined turquoise and vivid coral beads. All the elements have been tied together wonderfully with exactly the right amount of silver. The proportions are perfect and the finishing touches of the carved turquoise and silver leaves are charming.

● Approximate length 20cm (8in.)

BEAD STORE

- **A** Twenty 6mm turquoise rondelles
- **B** Two 8mm red coral barrels
- **C** Nine 4mm Swarovski Indian red bicones
- **D** Two 6mm Swarovski Indian red bicones
- **E** Two 8mm Karen hill tribe silver beads
- **F** Four 6mm Karen hill tribe silver discs
- **G** Eighteen 3mm Karen hill tribe silver bicones
- **H** One 12mm lampworked focal bead

You will also need:
- ● Beading wire
- ● Silver toggle clasp
- ● Two 2x2mm sterling silver crimp beads
- ● Two 3mm sterling silver crimp covers
- ● One 15mm turquoise leaf
- ● One 15mm sterling silver leaf

Pyrite and turquoise

Kim Booth ~ Aztec Gold

This striking piece is dominated by the bright pyrite ovals, which the artist has matched with a wonderful turquoise-splashed lampworked bead. The addition of the turquoise rounds harmonizes the bracelet. The mixture of bead shapes is fabulous and the scrolled clasp adds finesse.

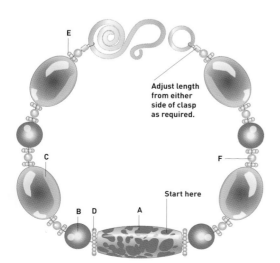

E

Adjust length from either side of clasp as required.

C

F

Start here

B D   A

● Approximate length 19cm (7½in.)

BEAD STORE

- **A** One 27mm lampworked bead
- **B** Four 8mm turquoise rounds
- **C** Four 18mm pyrite ovals
- **D** Two 9mm Bali silver spacers
- **E** Fourteen 4mm Bali silver daisy spacers
- **F** Eight 3mm sterling silver rounds

You will also need:
- ● One 25-cm (10-in.) length of Soft Flex beading wire
- ● Sterling silver hand-forged "S" clasp
- ● Two 2x2mm sterling silver crimp beads

Lapis lazuli and green aventurine

Gaile Almrott ~ Water's Edge

The strong colours of the lapis lazuli and the green aventurine are unified perfectly by the lampworked beads here, and the quantity of silver is exactly right for balance. The artist has skillfully kept the silver quite plain and all the beads to a similar size, for a perfectly proportioned bracelet that allows the gemstones to dominate.

● Approximate length 19.5cm (7¾in.)

BEAD STORE

A Six 8mm lapis lazuli rounds

B Four 8mm green aventurine rounds

C Three 12mm lampworked beads

D Six 6mm Karen hill tribe silver beads

E Eighteen 3mm Karen hill tribe silver spacers

F Four 8mm Karen hill tribe silver bead caps

G One 6mm green aventurine round

H Karen hill tribe silver leaf charm

I Karen hill tribe silver flower charm

You will also need:
● Beading wire
● Silver toggle clasp
● Two 2x2mm sterling silver crimp beads
● Two 3mm sterling silver crimp covers
● Long eye pin
● Closed jump ring

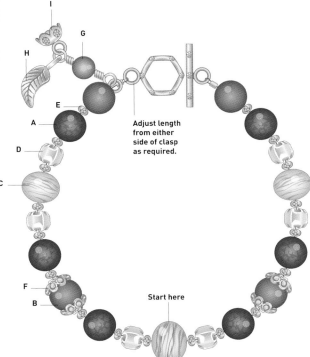

Adjust length from either side of clasp as required.

Start here

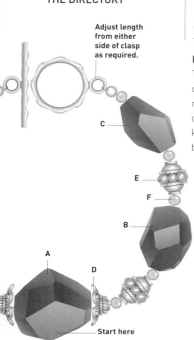

Adjust length from either side of clasp as required.

C

E

F

B

A

D

Start here

Smoky quartz

Kim Gover ~ Shadowkeeper

This bracelet is a bold, chunky piece. The smoky quartz nuggets are a lovely colour, and the faceting really enhances each stone, catching the light at different angles and casting shadows. Simplicity is the key here, with the large ornate silver beads and caps brightening the overall effect.

● Approximate length 19.5cm (7¾in.)

BEAD STORE

Ⓐ One 28x20mm faceted smoky quartz bead

Ⓑ Two 22x18mm faceted smoky quartz beads

Ⓒ Two 18x16mm faceted smoky quartz beads

Ⓓ Two lentil bead caps

Ⓔ Four 10x8mm Bali silver beads

Ⓕ Ten 3mm Karen hill tribe silver spacers

You will also need:
● Beading wire
● Silver toggle clasp
● Two 2x2mm sterling silver crimp beads
● Two 3mm sterling silver crimp covers

Tiger's eye

Terry West ~ Blue Galaxy

These large tiger's eye rounds have a fabulous depth of colour and an amazing sheen, and the artist has really allowed them to play the starring role in this gorgeous bracelet. The use of square bead caps on round beads is inspired, and the large ornate toggle clasp is a design feature that adds a flawless finish.

● Approximate length 21.5cm (8¼in.)

BEAD STORE

Ⓐ Five 20mm blue tiger's eye rounds

Ⓑ Ten 10x10mm square sterling silver bead caps

You will also need:
● Six 4-cm (1½-in.) lengths of 0.8mm (20-gauge) half-round, dead-soft sterling silver wire
● Large silver toggle clasp

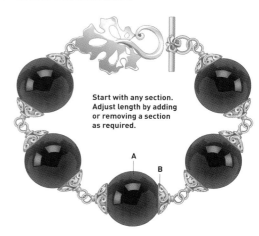

Start with any section. Adjust length by adding or removing a section as required.

A

B

Bronzite and Owyhee jasper

Kim Booth ~ Earthy Treasure

The rich chocolate-brown tones of the bronzite give warmth to this bracelet against the contrasting smoky greys of the Owyhee jasper. The filigree bead caps soften the lines of the rectangles, and teamed with the ornate silver beads provide a more dainty appearance. The patterned toggle completes the piece perfectly.

- Approximate length 19cm (7½in.)

BEAD STORE

A Three 20mm bronzite rectangles

B Six 8mm Owyhee jasper cubes

C Two 9mm Bali Silver beads

D Six 7mm sterling silver filigree bead caps

E Twelve 4mm sterling silver rounds

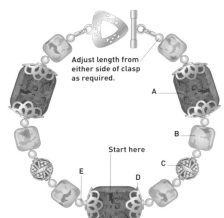

Adjust length from either side of clasp as required.

Start here

You will also need:

- 25-cm (10-in.) length of Soft Flex beading wire
- Bali silver toggle clasp
- Two 2x2mm sterling silver crimp beads
- Two small sterling silver wire guardians

Lava stone and onyx

Adjust length from either side of clasp as required.

Gaile Almrott ~ Duet

The artist has used three incredibly tactile lava stone beads as the focal point of this bracelet. These stones have an interesting texture and have been cleverly used with the smooth onyx discs to striking effect. The balance is perfect, with just the right amount of silver to add brightness.

- Approximate length 18.5cm (7¼in.)

BEAD STORE

A Three 10mm lava stone rounds

B Fourteen 10mm matte black onyx saucer beads

C Two 6mm Swarovski morion crystal bicones

D Two 4mm Swarovski morion crystal bicones

E Two 10mm sterling silver bead caps

F Four 8mm Karen hill tribe silver beads

G Eight 6mm Karen hill tribe silver discs

H Four 4mm Karen hill tribe silver spacer beads

Start here

You will also need:

- Beading wire
- Silver toggle clasp
- Two 2x2mm sterling silver crimp beads
- Two 3mm sterling silver crimp covers

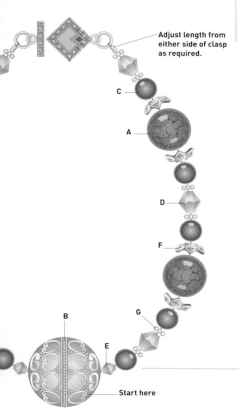

Adjust length from either side of clasp as required.

C

A

D

F

B

G

E

Start here

Ocean jasper

Lorna Prime ~ Riverbank

This earthy, organic bracelet features the lush, mossy-patterned ocean jasper. The artist has accented the colours in the gemstones perfectly with the olivine crystals and dark green pearls, and the ornate focal bead, caps, and toggle provide lift and sparkle as well as a slightly oriental feel.

● Approximate length 23cm (9in.)

BEAD STORE

Ⓐ Four 10mm ocean jasper rounds

Ⓑ One large Bali silver ornate round

Ⓒ Ten 6mm dark green glass pearls

Ⓓ Six 6mm Swarovski olivine bicones

Ⓔ Two 4mm Swarovski olivine bicones

Ⓕ Eight 8mm sterling silver bead caps

Ⓖ Twelve 4mm sterling silver daisy spacers

You will also need:
● Stringing material
● Silver toggle clasp
● Two 2x2mm sterling silver crimp beads

You will also need:
● 25-cm (10-in.) length of Soft Flex extreme beading wire
● Bali silver toggle clasp
● Two 2x2mm sterling silver crimp beads
● Two sterling silver wire guardians

Kambaba jasper and tourmaline

Kim Booth ~ Verdant

The rectangles used here are excellent examples of kambaba jasper, and the tourmaline crystals coordinate very well with the swirling colours contained within the rectangles. The oxidized silver bead caps and tubes provide a real vintage air to this elegant bracelet.

● Approximate length 19cm (7½in.)

BEAD STORE

Ⓐ Three 23mm kambaba jasper rectangles

Ⓑ Six Bali silver lentil bead caps

Ⓒ Four 6mm Bali pointed oval beads

Ⓓ Four 6mm Swarovski tourmaline bicones

Ⓔ Four 4mm Swarovski tourmaline bicones

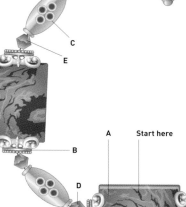

Adjust length from either side of clasp as required.

C

E

B

A

Start here

D

Jade

Vicki Honeywill ~ Berry Bracelet

The colours of the jade in this simply styled bracelet really "pop", and the addition of the silver tubes and spacer beads give it an ultra-modern feel. Striking in its simplicity, this is one bracelet you could wear for any occasion.

● Approximate length 20cm (8in.)

BEAD STORE

Ⓐ Five 8mm colourful jade rounds

Ⓑ Ten 4mm colourful jade rounds

Ⓒ Four 15mm sterling silver curved tube beads

Ⓓ Ten 4mm sterling silver daisy spacers

Ⓔ Eight 4mm Thai silver coiled beads

You will also need:
● Beading wire
● Thai silver toggle clasp
● Two 2x2mm crimp beads
● Two 4mm sterling silver crimp covers

Adjust length from either side of clasp as required.

A

E

C

B

D

Start here

Turquoise and coral

Terry McCarthy ~ Turquoise Treasure

This bracelet uses a variety of beads in different sizes and shapes: turquoise nuggets and chips, coral bicone beads, glass, silver, and painted wood beads. The free-hanging, colourful charm makes the bracelet extra special. The beads in this strung bracelet have so much character that they form the design themselves – only a couple of silver spacer beads and bead caps are needed to set it off.

● Approximate length 20cm (8in.)

BEAD STORE

- **A** Three large natural turquoise nuggets
- **B** Six 8mm yellow cat's eye rounds
- **C** One large mookaite nugget
- **D** Two 12mm painted wooden rounds
- **E** Eight 6mm coral bicones
- **F** Twelve natural turquoise chips
- **G** Three 7mm sterling silver bead caps
- **H** Three 5mm sterling silver daisy spacers
- **I** Three coral 4mm rounds
- **J** 1g of size 11 red seed beads
- **K** One sterling silver patterned bead

You will also need:

- Sterling silver 12mm toggle clasp
- Beading wire
- Crimp beads
- Sterling silver crimp covers
- Three 3mm sterling silver rounds
- 4-cm (1½-in.) length of sterling silver chain, 3x4mm link size
- Twelve 35mm sterling silver head pins

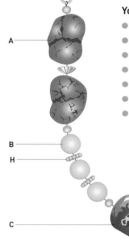

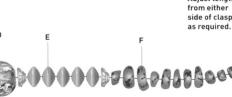

Start here

Adjust length from either side of clasp as required.

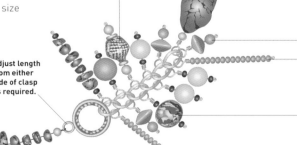

Black onyx

● Approximate length 19cm (7½in.)

BEAD STORE

(A) One dark green handmade lampworked glass bead, approximately 12x10mm

(B) Four 8mm black onyx rounds

(C) Six 6mm Swarovski crystal emerald bicones

(D) Two 4mm black onyx rounds

(E) Two Karen hill tribe silver curved tubes

(F) Four 8mm Karen hill tribe silver bead caps

(G) Four 6mm Karen hill tribe silver coiled beads

(H) Four 3mm sterling silver rounds

Vicki Honeywill ~ Dark Mystery

Handmade lampworked bead, black onyx, Austrian crystals, and Karen hill tribe silver are the special ingredients in this lovely bracelet. It is a real classic and will never go out of fashion. Unusually with a piece using so much silver, it has been strung and is balanced with just the right ratio of beads to silver in order to enhance the beauty of the beads.

You will also need:
● 11mm Karen hill tribe silver toggle clasp
● Beading wire
● 2x2mm sterling silver crimp beads
● 3mm sterling silver crimp covers

Adjust length from either side of clasp as required.

Mixed gemstones and silver

● Approximate length 19cm (7½in.)

BEAD STORE

(A) Twelve 8mm gemstone rounds

(B) 15mm silver lentil bead

(C) Two 4mm rounds

(D) Two 10mm hammered round rings

(E) Two 7mm silver beads

(F) Eight 8mm silver bead caps

(G) Eight 5mm silver daisy spacer beads

You will also need:
● Silver toggle clasp
● Beading wire
● 2x2mm sterling silver crimp beads
● 3mm sterling silver crimp covers

Anita Seeberg ~ Chakra

Simple elegance, using just round gemstone beads and silver. The beauty of the gemstones is really underlined in this design. The gemstones used include onyx, chrysoprase, golden jade, red garnet, and carnelian.

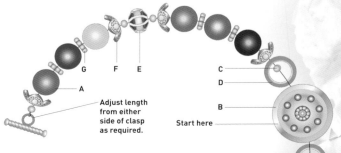

Adjust length from either side of clasp as required.

Start here

Earrings

Malachite

Diane Fairhall ~ Laura

These earrings really do have the "wow factor", and serve as timeless classics. A substantial rectangle of malachite with beautiful markings is offset with Bali silver bead caps, for earrings with impact.

BEAD STORE

(A) Two 12x18mm malachite rectangles

(B) Four Bali silver bead caps

You will also need:
- Pair of sterling silver flower ear wires
- Two eye pins

Apatite

Karin Chilton ~ Dew Drops

This ultra-feminine, pretty pair of chandelier earrings epitomizes summer chic. The beautiful sea green of the apatite is fresh and cool, and the scrolled silver adds brightness; the balance of beads to silver is spot on.

BEAD STORE

(A) Twenty 3–4mm apatite rounds

(B) Twenty-six 2mm sterling silver rounds

(C) Two sterling silver chandelier hangers

Chrysocolla, aragonite, and tourmaline

Kim Gover ~ The Dark Side of Citrus

These earrings contain citrus-coloured stones by way of apple green chrysocolla and lemon yellow aragonite. They have been teamed with unusual large black tourmaline barrels for a contrast that really enhances the vivid colours. Opal-coloured crystals have been included to aid the silver findings in creating lift and adding sparkle.

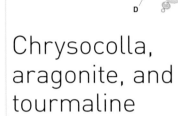

BEAD STORE

(A) Two 20x15mm black tourmaline grooved barrels

(B) Six 8mm aragonite rounds

(C) Six 6mm chrysocolla rounds

(D) Six 4mm Swarovski white opal bicones

(E) Two 6mm Swarovski white opal bicones

You will also need:
- Pair of sterling silver ear wires
- Two long sterling silver eye pins
- Two 5mm sterling silver bead caps
- Four 3mm Karen hill tribe silver spacers
- Ten 2mm sterling silver disc spacers

Azurite/malachite

Diane Fairhall ~ Alkanet

These earrings are a real statement in sophisticated splendour. The azurite part of the stone is an amazingly vivid blue, naturally intergrown with the malachite to stunning effect. The stacked graduated stones are simple in style but, teamed with the long threader posts, give an air of glamour.

BEAD STORE

- **A** Six 8mm azurite/malachite rondelles
- **B** Four 4mm azurite/malachite rondelles
- **C** Twelve 2mm sterling silver round beads

You will also need:
- Pair of sterling silver threader earrings
- Two long sterling silver head pins or a length of silver wire to string the beads onto

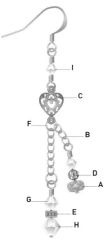

Mixed gemstones

Nan Fry ~ Autumn Fruits

This fresh and juicy pair of cluster earrings features mixed gemstones and is particularly stylish. The bright citrus colours of the peridot, jade, and carnelian are balanced with the rich earthy colours of the garnet, jasper, and topaz, which means that these earrings inspire thoughts of hot summer days with a glass of fruit punch.

BEAD STORE

- **A** Four 6mm smoky topaz rondelles
- **B** Two 8mm poppy jasper rounds
- **C** Two 6mm peridot rounds
- **D** Two 6mm jadeite rounds
- **E** Two 8mm faceted carnelian rounds
- **F** Two 6mm garnet ovals

You will also need:
- Pair of ear wires
- Twelve sterling silver head pins
- Two 3-link lengths of curb chain

Labradorite

Trudi Doherty ~ Cleopatra

Copper is an excellent choice of metal to partner the labradorite rondelles featured at the end of the chain section of these earrings. Soft blue accent crystals pick up the flashes of colour in this versatile gemstone, making a very fashionable pair of earrings.

BEAD STORE

- **A** Two 6mm faceted labradorite buttons
- **B** Two 9-link lengths of copper chain, 2.8mm (1/10in.) link size
- **C** Two copper filigree heart connectors
- **D** Two 4mm copper filigree balls
- **E** Two 4mm copper square spacers
- **F** Six 5mm copper jump rings
- **G** Four 5mm Swarovski Pacific opal bicones
- **H** Two 6mm Swarovski light sapphire AB bicones
- **I** Two 4mm Swarovski light sapphire bicones

You will also need:
- Pair of copper ear wires
- Copper wire to attach the hearts

Aragonite

Vicki Honeywill ~ Palest Primrose

Delicate and pretty, these stacked earrings are created with graduating sizes of aragonite rounds: opaque and milky with a hint of lemon, they have an ethereal quality. The style is uncomplicated but has versatility, so these earrings will take you through the day and on to an evening out on the town.

BEAD STORE

- **A** Two 8mm aragonite rounds
- **B** Two 6mm aragonite rounds
- **C** Two 4mm aragonite rounds
- **D** Eight 3mm sterling silver rounds

You will also need:
- Pair of sterling silver ear wires
- Two sterling silver head pins

Charoite

Kim Gover ~ Moorland Heather

The charoite coins in these earrings embrace myriad pastel colours. Simple but effective, the crystals in the dangle section at the base echo the colours of the stone, and the combination of the bicones paired with the large coins is appealing.

BEAD STORE

- (A) Two 20mm charoite coins
- (B) Two 3mm Bali silver daisy spacers
- (C) Eight 4mm Swarovski light amethyst bicones
- (D) Four 4mm Swarovski erinite bicones

You will also need:

- Pair of Bali silver ear wires
- Two long sterling silver eye pins
- Ten sterling silver head pins
- Two sterling silver lentil bead caps
- Two 5mm sterling silver split rings

Citrine

Kim Booth ~ Sunshine

These long, elegant dangle earrings elongate the neck and showcase beautiful faceted citrine in a lovely shade of honeyed lemon. The style is simple but very effective, the open design allows light to penetrate the stones, and the twisted rings also reflect the light back into the stone. Stylish, elegant, and a timeless classic.

BEAD STORE

- (A) Six 8mm faceted citrine beads

You will also need:

- Pair of sterling silver lever-back ear wires
- Four 5cm (2in.) 0.5mm (24-gauge) sterling silver eye pins
- Two 5cm (2in.) 0.5mm (24-gauge) sterling silver head pins
- Four 8mm sterling silver twisted closed jump rings

Serpentine

Peter Hoffman ~ Serpentine Donuts

These earrings are bound to get you noticed; the large serpentine donuts are real statement pieces and have fascinating veins and mottling running through them. The ornate Bali silver beads add balance to the overall design – simply beautiful.

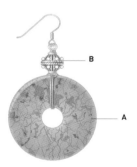

BEAD STORE

- (A) Two 40mm serpentine donuts
- (B) Two 8x7mm Bali silver ornate beads

You will also need:

- Pair of sterling silver ear wires
- Length of sterling silver wire for wrapping

Rhodochrosite

Kim Gover ~ Shimmer

This is a quirky pair of earrings, with the three sections combining different shapes. The cylinders and rectangles show just how different rhodochrosite can be in both colour and markings, while the crystals reflect some of the shades displayed in the bottom components.

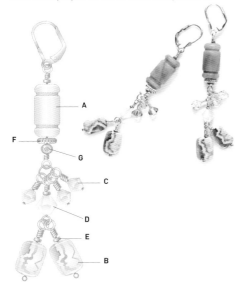

BEAD STORE

Ⓐ Two 16mm rhodochrosite tubes

Ⓑ Four 10x6mm rhodochrosite rectangles

Ⓒ Six 5mm Swarovski light rose bicones

Ⓓ Two 6mm Swarovski white opal bicones

Ⓔ Eight 2mm sterling silver disc spacers

Ⓕ Two 5mm sterling silver rope spacers

Ⓖ Two 3mm Karen hill tribe silver spacers

You will also need:

● Pair of sterling silver ear wires
● Four sterling silver eye pins
● Ten sterling silver head pins

Mother-of-pearl

Heather Marrow ~ Hocus Pocus

This dramatic pair of earrings makes excellent use of smoky grey, lustrous mother-of-pearl, and are reminiscent of the moon hiding behind clouds. The silver scrollwork highlights the pearl, the curving forms echoing the line of the central discs, and the ornate filigree caps round everything off perfectly.

Create the scrolled components first (see "creating the scrolls", below).

BEAD STORE

Ⓐ Two 30mm mother-of-pearl coins

Ⓑ Four 4x6mm faceted jet rondelles

Ⓒ Two 8mm filigree bead caps

You will also need:

● Pair of sterling silver ear wires
● Two sterling silver head pins
● Two 18cm (7in.) lengths of 1.6mm (14-gauge) silver wire for the scrolled sections
● Total of 10cm (4in.) of 0.5mm (24-gauge) silver wire to secure the scrolls in place

CREATING THE SCROLLS

Mark the centre of the 1.6mm (14-gauge) wire and create loops at each end facing each other. Bend the wire in half and pinch to tighten the loop at the centre. Form the loops at each end into spirals, taking care to keep them even until approximately 3cm (1¼in.) long. Bend the middle loop at a 90-degree angle to form a lip. This component is now ready to be incorporated into the design.

Mother-of-pearl and jet

Heather Marrow ~ Abra Cadabra

The mother-of-pearl used here shimmers like the moon, and is set with delicate faceted jet beads, creating wonderful contrast. The scrolled copper sections bring warmth and a sculptural quality to this desirable pair of earrings.

BEAD STORE

Ⓐ Two 30mm mother-of-pearl coins

Ⓑ Four 4x6mm faceted jet rondelles

Ⓒ Four 4mm Bali-style copper spacers

You will also need:

● Pair of copper ear wires
● Two 0.7mm (21-gauge) copper fancy head pins
● Two 18cm (7in.) lengths of 1.6mm (14-gauge) copper wire for the scrolled sections
● Total of 10cm (4in.) of 0.5mm (24-gauge) copper wire to secure the scrolls in place

Create the scrolled components first (see "creating the scrolls", below).

Matching Sets

Picture jasper

Lorna Prime/Pixie Willow Designs ~ Shifting Sands

Fabulous picture jasper with its myriad sandy striations is the focus of this lovely set. The artist has teamed these stones with glass pearls and kept other components to a minimum by using sections of sterling silver wire to create focal curlicues and an "S" clasp. The use of the chain neckpiece maintains simple elegance and allows the gemstones to draw the eye.

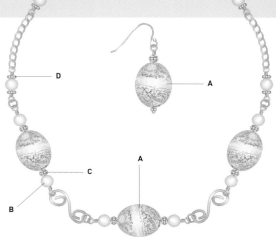

Adjust chain length as required.

D   A

C

A

B

Create components first, then string from the centre.

You will also need:

- Eight 5mm (⅛in.) sterling silver closed jump rings
- 2.5-cm (2-in.) length of 0.5mm (24-gauge) sterling silver half-hard wire
- Two 2.5-cm (2-in.) lengths of 1.0mm (18-gauge) sterling silver half-hard wire
- Sterling silver chain

BEAD STORE

Necklace

- Approximate length 44cm (17⅓in.)

Ⓐ Three 20mm picture jasper ovals

Ⓑ Twelve 6mm cream glass pearls

Ⓒ Six 4mm Bali silver ornate spacers

Ⓓ Twelve 4mm sterling silver spacers

Earrings

Ⓐ Two large picture jasper ovals

You will also need:

- Pair of sterling silver ear wires
- Two Bali silver fancy head pins
- Two 4mm Bali silver ornate spacers

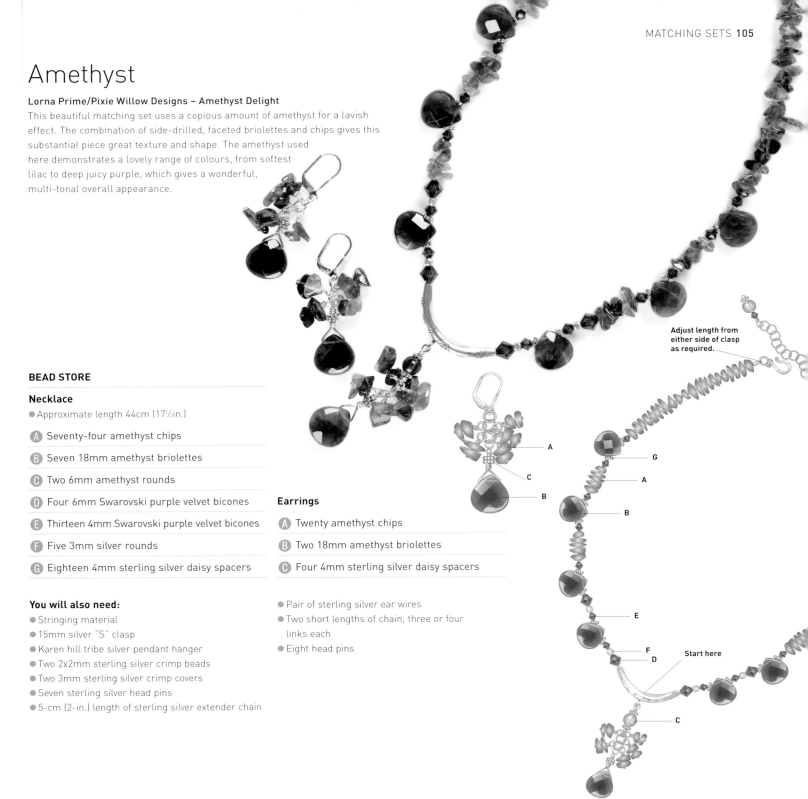

Amethyst

Lorna Prime/Pixie Willow Designs ~ Amethyst Delight

This beautiful matching set uses a copious amount of amethyst for a lavish effect. The combination of side-drilled, faceted briolettes and chips gives this substantial piece great texture and shape. The amethyst used here demonstrates a lovely range of colours, from softest lilac to deep juicy purple, which gives a wonderful, multi-tonal overall appearance.

BEAD STORE

Necklace

● Approximate length 44cm (17⅓in.)

A Seventy-four amethyst chips

B Seven 18mm amethyst briolettes

C Two 6mm amethyst rounds

D Four 6mm Swarovski purple velvet bicones

E Thirteen 4mm Swarovski purple velvet bicones

F Five 3mm silver rounds

G Eighteen 4mm sterling silver daisy spacers

You will also need:

● Stringing material
● 15mm silver "S" clasp
● Karen hill tribe silver pendant hanger
● Two 2x2mm sterling silver crimp beads
● Two 3mm sterling silver crimp covers
● Seven sterling silver head pins
● 5-cm (2-in.) length of sterling silver extender chain

Earrings

A Twenty amethyst chips

B Two 18mm amethyst briolettes

C Four 4mm sterling silver daisy spacers

● Pair of sterling silver ear wires
● Two short lengths of chain, three or four links each
● Eight head pins

Adjust length from either side of clasp as required.

Start here

Chrysoprase and pearl

Karin Chilton ~ Mint Julep

This cool and refreshing set comprises green chrysoprase and baroque
freshwater pearls teamed with sterling silver accents. The necklace is a lovely,
easy-to-wear Y-style, with a dangle drop focal, bringing interest to the neckline.
The bracelet is well balanced with a cute dangle accent to the clasp, and the
tasteful earrings are an excellent addition to the ensemble.

BEAD STORE

Necklace
● Approximate length 43cm (17in.)

(A) Twenty-one 12x11mm chrysoprase ovals

(B) Ten 8mm baroque white freshwater pearls

(C) Twenty-four 2mm sterling silver rounds

(D) Thirty-six 4mm sterling silver daisy spacers

(E) Five 7mm Karen hill tribe silver swirl beads

(F) One 10mm Karen hill tribe silver heart bead

(G) Two 8mm Karen hill tribe silver textured rounds

You will also need:
● Stringing material
● Sterling silver 10mm trigger clasp
● Two sterling silver calottes
● Two 6mm sterling silver jump rings

Bracelet
● Approximate length 19cm (7½in.)

(A) Three 12x11mm chrysoprase ovals

(B) Nine 8mm baroque white freshwater pearls

(C) Two 8mm Karen hill tribe silver textured rounds

(D) Seventeen 2mm sterling silver rounds

(E) Six 4mm sterling silver daisy spacers

You will also need:
● Beading wire
● 15mm Karen hill tribe silver rose clasp
● Four 2x2mm sterling silver crimp beads
● Four 3mm sterling silver crimp covers

**Create dangle, then
string from centre.**

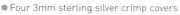

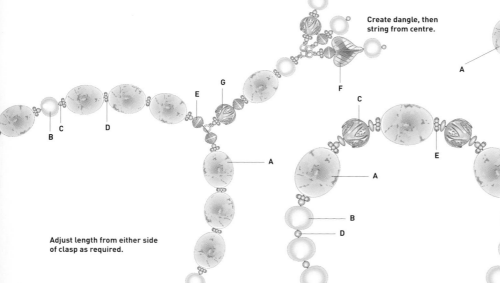

**Adjust length from either side
of clasp as required.**

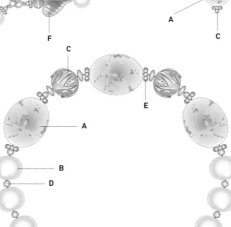

Earrings

(A) Two 12x11mm chrysoprase ovals

(B) Two 8mm baroque white freshwater pearls

(C) Four 4mm sterling silver daisy spacers

(D) Six 2mm sterling silver rounds

● Pair of sterling silver ear wires
● Four sterling silver head pins

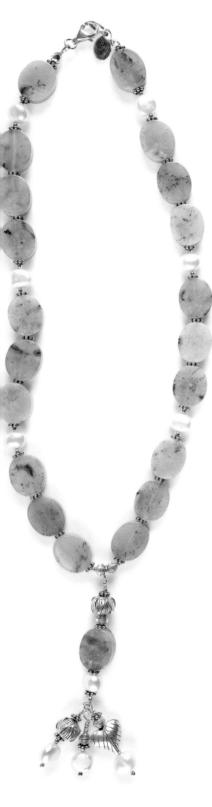

Jet and coral

Terry West ~ Jet Set

This striking set has an ethnic feel to it. The carved jet has an almost tribal essence, and the artist has used red coral to offset it wonderfully. The ornate silver beads have been used in exactly the right quantity to harmonize the pieces, while the oxidization in them also complements the jet. Both the bracelet and the earrings are perfectly proportioned, making a highly desirable duo.

BEAD STORE

Bracelet

● Approximate length 19.5cm (7¾in.)

A One 25x20mm carved jet bead

B Two 15x10mm carved jet beads

C Eighteen 6mm red coral discs

D One 15mm red coral teardrop

E Four 10x5mm sterling silver tubes

F Six 7mm sterling silver rope spacers

G Two 8mm sterling silver open swirl beads

You will also need:

● Beading wire
● 15mm Sterling silver toggle clasp
● 10mm sterling silver dangle charm
● Two 2x2mm sterling silver crimp beads
● Two sterling silver wire guardians

Earrings

A Two 15x10mm carved jet beads

B Four 6mm red coral discs

C Two 25x20mm jet teardrops

D Two 8mm sterling silver open swirl beads

You will also need:

● Pair of sterling silver lever-back ear wires
● Two sterling silver ornate connectors
● 10-cm (4-in.) length of 0.6mm (22-gauge) sterling silver wire for wrapping the loops top and bottom

D
A
B
C

D
E
C
F
B
G
A

Adjust length from either side of clasp as required.

Start here

Tiger's eye

Kim Gover ~ Tiger Tiger

Tiger's eye reigns supreme in this necklace and bracelet combination. The bracelet is substantial and incorporates lampworked beads with swirling tiger stripes. The looping of the two strands around the focal beads is innovative and adds depth to the design, creating a wide cuff style. The necklace keeps the set simple by echoing just one section of its counterpart.

Adjust length from either side of clasp as required.

Start here (see "Looping sequence", right).

Start here (see "Looping sequence", right).

BEAD STORE

Necklace

● Approximate length 43cm (17in.)

Ⓐ Eight 10mm tiger's eye rounds

Ⓑ Four 8mm tiger's eye rounds

Ⓒ Twelve 10x6mm tiger's eye ovals

Ⓓ Eight 6mm tiger's eye rounds

Ⓔ Six 12mm porcelain discs

Ⓕ One 18x14mm lampworked bead

Ⓖ Ten 6mm Swarovski smoked topaz bicones

Ⓗ Six 4mm Swarovski topaz bicones

Ⓘ Twenty 3mm Karen hill tribe silver spacers

You will also need:

● Stringing material
● 10mm Karen hill tribe silver toggle clasp
● Two 2x2mm sterling silver crimp beads
● Two 3mm sterling silver crimp covers

Bracelet

● Approximate length 19.5cm (7¾in.)

Ⓐ Five 10mm tiger's eye rounds

Ⓑ Two 8mm tiger's eye rounds

Ⓒ Thirty-two 6mm tiger's eye rounds

Ⓓ Four 18x14mm lampworked beads

Ⓔ Twenty-four 4mm Swarovski topaz bicones

Ⓕ Two 6mm Swarovski smoked topaz rounds

Ⓖ Two 3mm Karen hill tribe silver spacers

You will also need:

● Stringing material
● 10mm sterling silver toggle clasp
● Two 2x2mm sterling silver crimp beads
● Two 3mm sterling silver crimp covers

Looping sequence

Use two wires through the central stone, and string a crystal on all four exposed ends. Take one wire feed on four beads, loop around the focal and back through the crystal on the opposite end of the wire, then back through the focal. Repeat on the other side and feed a crystal over both strands on each side. Use the same sequence for the bracelet, repeated four times.

Amber and picture jasper

Kim Gover ~ Amber Lights

The earthy tone and pattern of the picture jasper interspersed with the deep rich honey of the amber give this Y-style necklace and coordinating bracelet an organic feel. This well-balanced set is versatile enough to be worn with a variety of styles.

BEAD STORE

Necklace

- Approximate length 42cm (16½in.)

A Seven 6mm amber rounds

B Seventeen 10x7mm picture jasper ovals

C Ten 6mm Bali silver bead caps

D One 25-mm (1-in.) length of sterling silver chain

E Three 8mm Bali silver floral beads

F Thirty-four 3mm sterling silver beads

You will also need:

- Beading wire
- Silver "S" clasp
- Four 2x2mm sterling silver crimp beads
- Four 3mm sterling silver crimp covers
- 4mm split ring
- Three sterling silver head pins
- Sterling silver eye pin

Bracelet

- Approximate length 19cm (7½in.)

A Four 6mm amber rounds

B Five 10x7mm picture jasper ovals

C Eight 6mm Bali silver bead caps

D Eight 6mm Swarovski light azore bicones

E Ten 3mm Karen hill tribe silver spacers

You will also need:

- Beading wire
- Silver toggle clasp
- Two 2x2mm sterling silver crimp beads
- Two 3mm sterling silver crimp covers

Start here by crimping two lengths of wire.

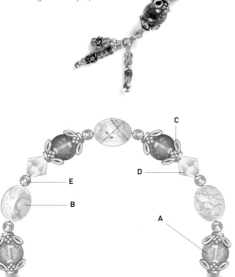

Other Accessories

Pearl

Kanina Wolff ~ La Lune

This ring is especially eye-catching, and makes a bold statement on the hand. It combines a very classic stone with modern, fashionable wire wrapping for a simple but striking look. Definitely a piece you would want to wear often.

BEAD STORE

(A) One 10mm freshwater ivory pearl semi-coin

You will also need:

- One 15cm (6in.) length of 1mm (18-gauge) sterling silver wire (increase length to enlarge ring size)
- One 63cm (25in.) length of 0.5mm (24-gauge) sterling silver wire

Making the pearl ring

1. Make a small loop in one end of the 15cm (6in.) length of wire.

2. Make the ring section by wrapping the length twice around a mandrel to the desired size.

3. Bend the first loop so it is at a 90-degree angle to the ring, and place the pearl against it.

4. Make another loop at the other end of the wire to hold the pearl snugly.

5. Take 63cm (25in.) of wire and coil it around the ring three times close to one of the loops. Thread it through the first loop, the pearl, and then the other loop. Wrap the wire around the other side of the ring three times.

6. Finish by wrapping the rest of the wire around the base of the pearl.

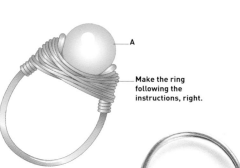

A

Make the ring following the instructions, right.

Coral

Anita Seeberg ~ Coral Reef

Simple in design but high in style, this great brooch has been created using coral beads in a rich red and a beautiful denim blue, with the addition of a jewellery safety pin. The asymmetric design is eye-catching; you could pin this to a jacket or a soft bag for a modern edge.

BEAD STORE

(A) Three 8mm blue sponge coral rounds

(B) One 8mm red coral round

(C) One 6mm Karen hill tribe silver coiled bead

(D) Two 8mm Karen hill tribe silver washer-style spacer beads

You will also need:

- Silver-plated 6cm (2.5in.) jewellery safety pin

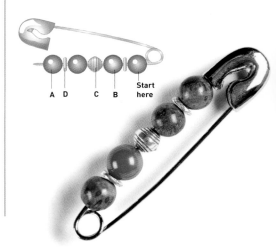

A D   C   B

Start here

Rhodonite

Anita Seeberg ~ Romance

This pin could be used as a brooch or a hat pin, or even on a soft purse. It is delicate and feminine in style, and the artist has used very pretty, deep pink rhodonite teamed with crystal and glass accent beads. The balance is perfect and the style won't date, making this piece an alluring addition to an accessory collection.

BEAD STORE

Ⓐ Three 4mm rhodonite rounds

Ⓑ One 8mm rhodonite round

Ⓒ One 15mm Karen hill tribe silver heart bead

Ⓓ One 6mm Swarovski light rose bicone

Ⓔ One 6mm Czech glass light pink bicone

Ⓕ One 6mm Karen hill tribe silver coiled bead

You will also need:

● Silver brooch or hat pin with loop

● Five sterling silver head pins

● 5-cm (2-in.) length of sterling silver chain (approximately 4mm [⅛in.] per link)

● 10-cm (4-in.) length of sterling silver 0.6mm (22-gauge) half-hard wire.

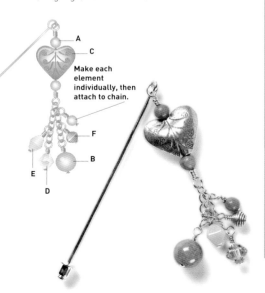

Goldstone and malachite

Kim Gover ~ Heart of Gold

This quirky charm could be hung from a purse or the belt loop of a pair of jeans. The distinctive, dark striped malachite enhances the bright, shimmering goldstone, which really catches the light. Making charms is a great way to try out, or use up, small quantities of gemstone beads.

BEAD STORE

Ⓐ Five 10mm red goldstone hearts

Ⓑ Five 6mm red goldstone rounds

Ⓒ Six 8mm malachite rounds

Ⓓ Four 6mm pale green glass rounds

Ⓔ Seven 3mm metal spacers

You will also need:

● Ten silver-plated head pins

● 5-cm (2-in.) length of silver-plated chain

● 8mm silver-plated twisted jump ring

● Swivel lever catch

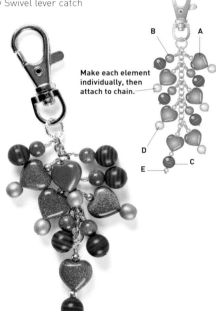

Make each element individually, then attach to chain.

Peridot and mother-of-pearl

Colette Ladley ~ Spring Love

A real hint of spring, this charm contains lovely fresh peridot chips, which the artist has teamed with a pretty polymer clay sunflower. The contrasting colours serve to make all the components stand out vividly. The whole piece is very tactile with its many strands of peridot.

BEAD STORE

Ⓐ Fifty small peridot chips

Ⓑ One 10mm flat shell bead

Ⓒ One 10mm flat mother-of-pearl heart

Ⓓ One 20mm red sunflower polymer clay bead

You will also need:

● Large swivel clasp

● Seven large links of sturdy chain

● 10mm silver-plated jump ring

● Ten silver-plated head pins.

Make each element individually, then attach to chain.

Chapter three
CORE TECHNIQUES

This chapter includes illustrated step-by-step techniques for stringing beads and using wire and metal findings, including simple knots, sterling silver findings, crimp beads, spacers, and wire twists, and zigzags.

Core Techniques

Simple wire loops

Simple loops are a good choice if you are new to working with wire, and they are perfectly adequate for securing a few beads on an earring. You should consider the weight of your beads to assess the strength of wire you require.

Tools and materials
- Wire
- Wire cutters
- Pliers: round-nosed and flat-nosed
- Two ear wires

1 Use wire cutters to cut two pieces of wire, allowing yourself plenty of length. Position round-nosed pliers about 5mm (³⁄₁₆in.) from the end of one length of wire and use them to bend the wire towards you to 45 degrees.

2 Move the pliers to the top of the wire and, using their tips, roll the wire away from you to form a small, neat loop. If required, place the pliers back into the loop to neaten and centralize it. The size of the loop depends on which part of the pliers is used. Here the tip is being used to make a very small loop.

3 Using flat-nosed pliers or your fingers, smooth down the wire a few times. This will strengthen and straighten it.

Individual closed-wire loops

These closed loops produce a very secure and professional-looking finish.
You should consider the weight of your beads to assess the strength of
wire you require.

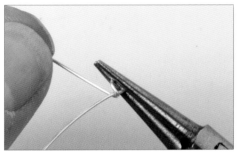

Tools and materials
- Wire
- Wire cutters
- Pliers: round-nosed and flat-nosed
- Two ear wires

1 Cut two lengths of wire, allowing at least 6cm (2½in.) more than the length of your bead or beads. Place round-nosed pliers onto the wire and rotate them anticlockwise to create a loop, allowing for a tail of excess wire to close the loop with. You will need to experiment to create the size of loop that is best for the beads you are using, and the length of wire you will need to close the loop.

2 Hold the wire by placing the pliers across the loop and use your finger and thumb to wind the tail end of the wire around the wire beneath the loop. You need to hold the wire firmly, but be careful not to let the pliers mark it.

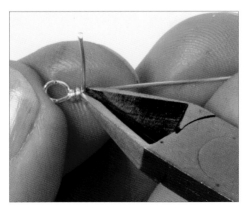

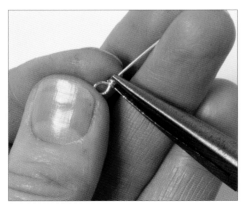

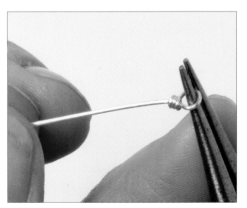

3 When you have wound the wire two or three times, clip the excess off as neatly as you can with wire cutters.

4 Use flat-nosed pliers to gently squeeze the sharp end of the wire back into the coils you have just formed. You have made a closed loop to secure your beads.

5 Put the round-nosed pliers back into the loop and use your fingers to straighten the wire and centralize the loop.

Using head pins and eye pins

For this example eye pins have been used with some small beads that complement the main bead. Thread the beads onto a eye pin. Use wire cutters to cut the excess wire at the top of the eye pin, ensuring there is 8mm (⁵⁄₁₆in.) of wire left above the beads. Make a simple wire loop (see page 114) at the top of the beads. Take an ear wire and use the pliers to open the loop sideways a little. Place the loop of the drop earring into the ear-wire loop, and use the pliers to close it up.

ear wire

simple loop

eye pin

Double hook and eye

This clasp works on the same principle as closed loops (see page 115). It is a sturdy clasp and can be used with chain, jump rings, or a matching "eye".

Tools and materials
- Wire: 0.6mm (22-gauge) or 0.8mm (20-gauge)
- Wire cutters
- Pliers: round-nosed and flat-nosed
- Two small beads

Other uses of wire loops

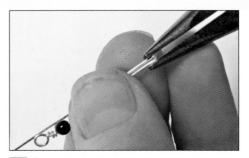

Closed-loop chain

By using closed loops you can create a chain of linked sections of beads that can't be pulled apart.

Closed-loop pendant

You will often come across items, with holes that go from front to back, that you might like to hang flat as a pendant or as earrings.

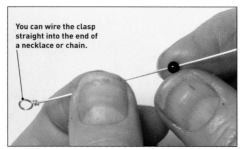

You can wire the clasp straight into the end of a necklace or chain.

1 Cut a length of wire, dependent on the size of hook that you want to achieve, although 12cm (4¾in.) is a good length to try initially. Make a closed loop at the bottom of the wire following the instructions for Individual Closed Loops on page 115. Thread on one bead.

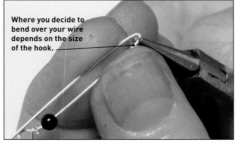

Where you decide to bend over your wire depends on the size of the hook.

2 Run your fingers along the wire to straighten and strengthen it. Hold the wire with the tip of the round-nosed pliers and bend it back on itself.

3 Press the doubled end closely together with flat-nosed pliers and smooth the wire back on itself with your fingers until you are a little way from the bead.

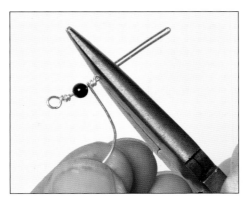

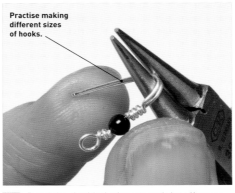

4 Still holding the doubled wire firmly in the pliers, create a right angle with the remaining length of wire. Wind this length of wire back down to the bead. Clip the extra length, and flatten the end.

5 Bend the doubled wire around the pliers to create a hook shape.

Practise making different sizes of hooks.

6 Angle the doubled wire a little, until it aligns with the closed loop.

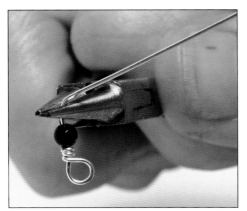

7 To make the eye, repeat the first step with a similar length of wire, then place the pliers horizontally across the wire above the bead and bend the wire towards you.

8 Adjust the angle of the pliers to the wire and wind the wire around the lower arm twice.

Try to match the size of the "eye" to the hook.

9 Hold these loops gently with the pliers and wind the wire back down towards the bead. Clip off the excess length and flatten the end with flat-nosed pliers.

Wrapping individual beads

This is an easy way to embellish a plain bead, using wires and a few other beads.

Tools and materials
- Wire: 0.8mm (20-gauge) (3 x the length of bead) and 0.6mm (22-gauge) (12 x the length of bead)
- Wire cutters
- Pliers: round-nosed and flat-nosed

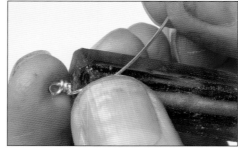

Fit the spiral inside the hole in the bead if possible.

1 Cut a length of 0.8mm (20-gauge) wire. Make a closed loop (see page 115). Now cut a long length of 0.6mm (22-gauge) wire. Use the round-nosed pliers to make a tiny spiral at the end of this length. Slide the spiral over the thicker wire and thread both of them into the bead, from the bottom.

2 Holding everything very firmly in your hand, start to wrap the 0.6mm (22-gauge) wire around the bead. When you have made one wrap, thread some of the small beads onto the wire and continue to wrap, spacing the beads into the wraps as you work.

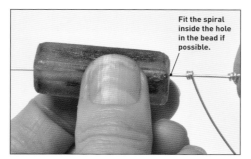

Hold and wrap as tightly as you can.

3 When you reach the top of the bead, wrap the wire as firmly around the bead as possible, then move the thinner wire back onto the thicker wire and wind around this a few times. Clip off the extra length and flatten in the end.

4 Push this spiral as close into the bead as you can, then add another bead to the 0.8mm (20-gauge) wire and make a closed loop above it. Trim the wire and flatten in the end.

Wire on wire wrapping

Wrapping with two different wires will create other decorative results. Start in the same way but attach a third, longer length of finer wire to the wrapping wire. Wrap this around the main wrapping wire as you wind up the main bead. Finish off in the same way as shown here.

5 To tighten the wire around the beads, use the tips of flat-nosed pliers against the wire and turn each wrap to make an angle in the wire. Do this as many times as you like, making sure you don't damage the bead or the wire. Be careful not to over-tighten to the extent that the wire snaps.

Coils

These can be used as decorative head pins for drop earrings or incorporated into other designs.

Tools and materials
- Wire
- Wire cutters
- Pliers: round-nosed and flat-nosed

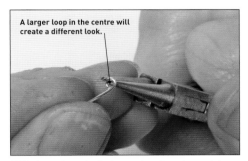

A larger loop in the centre will create a different look.

1 Cut a length of wire and make a loop with the smallest point of the round-nosed pliers.

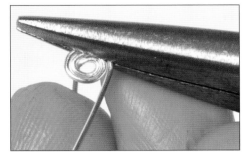

2 Position the flat-nosed pliers across the loop to hold it firmly, but without marking the wire. Use your fingers to wind the length of wire around the loop to create a coil.

3 The coil can be finished with a simple loop, as shown here, or a closed loop.

Zigzag spacers

Zigzag spacers work well in either earrings or necklaces. This is an excellent design with which to experiment with hammering. Ideally you need a small block to hammer onto, and you need a small hammer, but it is fine to experiment with household tools and smooth surfaces.

Tools and materials
- Wire
- Wire cutters
- Pliers: round-nosed and flat-nosed
- Hammer and block (optional)

1 Cut two lengths of wire and put one aside to be used as a measure. Make a loop at the end around round-nosed pliers. Move the pliers along a little further and turn the wire back onto itself.

2 Continue to turn the wire in the same way so it zigzags from side to side. At the end of the zigzag, make a final turn back so that you create a loop that turns back into the zigzag. Clip off the excess wire.

3 Hammer the spacer, if desired, to give extra strength. This will slightly increase its size, so you may want to re-scale your design before making more. The spacers can be linked with simple or closed loops.

Knotting onto a clasp

This is an easy way to attach a clasp without findings or specialist tools. This method can be used for beads that won't take two thicknesses of thread.

Tools and Materials
- Beading needle
- Blunt needle
- Clasp

Use a needle with a large enough "eye".

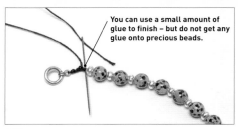

You can use a small amount of glue to finish – but do not get any glue onto precious beads.

1 Thread the beads, allowing about 15cm (6in.) of extra thread at each side. Make a half knot in the thread close to the beads and place a blunt needle in it. Now position the clasp about 1cm (⅜in.) from the knot.

2 Make a knot next to the clasp by working the short thread over the main thread and back through the loop. Tighten the knot. Repeat these knots down to the knot with the needle in it, making each one tight and even.

3 Work the end of the thread through its knot using the needle. This will give you knots working in two different directions. Thread the end back down as many of the beads as you can and trim. Repeat on the other side.

Calottes

The more flexible varieties of beading wires can be knotted at the ends, or between beads. These can be attached to the clasp using a calotte over the knot at the end of the strand. This is also a simple way to attach several strands of beads to a clasp.

Tools and materials
- Beading wire
- Wire cutters or very heavy-duty scissors
- Tape (optional)
- Two calottes
- Flat-nosed pliers
- Blunt needle
- Clasp

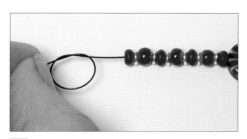

Look for the little groove in the calotte for the thread to sit in.

1 Thread your beads. Make an overhand knot in the other end of the wire.

2 Place the knot into a calotte and use flat-nosed pliers to gently squeeze it over the knot.

3 At the other end, make a knot and put a blunt needle into it. Use the needle to slide the knot close, but not too close, to the beads. Squeeze another calotte over this knot.

Knotting into a clamshell calotte

Although the use of calottes is featured opposite, the use of clamshell calottes to attach a clasp is slightly different because the beading thread is knotted through these findings.

Tools and materials
- 2 clamshell calottes
- Round-nosed pliers
- Beading needle
- Blunt needle
- Clasp

Open the loops sideways.

1 Cut a length of thread, allowing an extra 4–5cm (1¾–2in.) on each side for finishing. Make a secure knot in one end. Thread on the clamshell calotte. Trim the thread. Close the calotte over the knot. Thread on the beads.

2 Thread the other clamshell calotte. Make another double overhand knot and put a blunt needle into the knot. Draw the knot down towards the calotte, tightening it as it moves.

3 Close the calotte over the knot as before. Gently roll the loops on the calottes over the loops on your chosen clasp.

Crimping

When working with the new specialist threading materials, such as tiger tail and other similar beading wires, you will need to learn how to crimp the ends of your work to attach a clasp.

Tools and materials
- Wire cutters or very heavy-duty scissors
- Tape (optional)
- Crimping pliers or flat-nosed pliers

1 Cut a length of beading wire, allowing 3–4cm (1¼–1½in.) extra at each end to attach the clasp, using wire cutters or heavy-duty scissors – good scissors will be spoiled by the wire. Thread on your beads. Thread a crimp on one end of the wire, then thread the wire through the clasp.

2 Thread the beading wire back through the crimp, leaving a loop that allows movement but looks neat. Use two crimps if you have heavy beads.

3 Flatten the crimp with crimping pliers. Slide the beads up to meet the crimp, passing them over the loose end of the thread if possible; if not, cut the loose end close to the crimp. Crimp the other end of the wire and attach the clasp, allowing for some movement.

Calottes on a multi-strand piece

A larger calotte works well over knots or crimps to join several strands together in a necklace or bracelet.

Tools and materials
- Multi-strand necklace or bracelet
- Crimps
- Wire cutters or heavy-duty scissors
- Tape (optional)
- Two calottes
- Flat-nosed pliers and crimping pliers
- Clasp

1 Use two crimps to attach the strands of the piece together. Clip the ends of the threads, then put a calotte around them.

2 Squeeze the calotte together with flat-nosed pliers. Close it firmly enough to hold the strands in place without shearing them. Repeat on the other side and attach a clasp.

Finishing multi-strands into a cone

Another approach when using many strands is to gather the ends together into a cone. You could finish with knots or crimps inside the cone.

Tools and materials
- Strands of beads
- Crimps
- Flat-nosed pliers or crimping pliers
- Beading wire
- Wire cutters or heavy-duty scissors
- Two cones
- Clasp

Make your strands of beads and check that they will hang well together.

1 Use crimps to secure the ends of your strands of beads, making small loops at the end of each thread. Cut a length of beading wire and make a simple loop at the end. Thread the wire through the loop on each strand of beads, then through the loop at the end of the wire. Repeat at the other end.

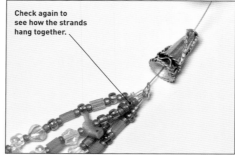

Check again to see how the strands hang together.

2 Now put a cone at each end of the necklace over all of the ends of the strands. Thread more beads onto each of the single threads and crimp them onto a clasp.

Threading variations

More examples of different ways in which beads can be threaded.

Y necklaces

This different shape for necklaces uses a single strand of wire or thread.

1 Cut a length of beading wire or thread, remembering to allow plenty of length for the drop. Start from the middle with a tiny, but strong, bead. Then bring the threads together through the central beads, so that the tiny bead will hold them in place.

Once these threads have been tightened, the beads will not be able to be repositioned.

2 Separate the threads when you have enough beads on the central drop. Choose some small beads for each strand first so that they will sit well together.

Double-strand threading

This is a way to use two separate strands of beading wire or thread together to make the beads sit in a different direction. It is useful for bracelets or chokers.

1 Cut two lengths of beading wire or thread, two to three times the length of the bracelet that you intend to make, depending on the length of the beads you are using. Crimp both threads to a clasp at one end. Separate the strands and add enough beads to cover them before you thread into the first bead from either side.

2 Add a few more small beads to cover the threads between the beads, and thread into the next bead from either end. Continue in this way, crossing the threads inside the beads until you reach your desired length and you can finish off in the same way that you started.

Resources

Online

www.crystalgems.co.uk
Information regarding crystal and gemstone properties and how they can be used with chakras and as remedies.

www.beadingtimes.com
Excellent source of information on all aspects of jewellery design. Updated monthly.

www.beadingdaily.com
Site containing projects, information, contests, galleries, and chat.

www.jewelinfo4u.com
A vast source of information ranging from gemstone data to tools required for jewellery making and designer galleries.

www.beadmagazine.co.uk
Site with projects, galleries, and forums. Also features *Bead TV*, showing tutorials, workshops, and demonstrations.

www.wire-sculpture.com
Excellent resource centre on wire and metal skills, containing projects and ideas as well as information on pricing and marketing your work.

www.conniefox.com/Education/Education.htm
Video jewellery tutorials on wire and metal skills and supplies for sale.

www.enijewelry.com
Amazing online tutorials on wire work; either pay to download the individual projects you require, or follow free links to beginners' lessons.

www.beadworkersguild.org.uk
A membership site publishing a journal and a selection of books, as well as running workshops and beading events.

www.beadersshowcase.com
An online community with a place to showcase your work and chat to other members with groups catering to all types of beading who will offer challenging projects to stimulate your creativity.

www.maillequeen.co.uk
Kits and tutorials for maille work.

Retailers

www.firemountain.com
An excellent online retailer with a huge range of gemstones and other supplies as well as a useful "encycloBEADia", gallery, and tutorials section.

www.auntiesbeads.com
Online retailer with a wide range of beads and findings as well as resources for weekly projects and free video tutorials.

www.merchantsoverseas.com
Information on all things Swarovski, with colour, shape, and size charts, seasonal colour trends, and an online retail area.

www.abeadstore.com
A selection of simple beading projects, tips, FAQs, and a retail area.

Books

It's All About the Beads, Barbara Case
David & Charles, 2006,
ISBN: 978-0715322840.
Step-by-step jewellery projects ranging from novice to expert ability covering a wide range of techniques.

The Beader's Colour Mixing Directory, Sandra Wallace
Search Press Ltd, 2007,
ISBN: 978-1844482153.
Inspirational themes, an explanation of colour mixing, and a selection of projects.

The Art and Elegance of Beadweaving: New Jewelry Designs with Classic Stitches, Carol Wilcox Wells
Search Press Ltd, 2002,
ISBN: 978-1903975251.
This book covers stitches and techniques used in beadweaving with clear diagrams and great photography.

Magazines

Beadstyle
www.beadstylemag.com
Excellent bi-monthly magazine with tutorials and supply lists incorporating a wide range of materials.

Bead and Button
www.beadandbutton.com
A magazine packed with loads of projects to challenge and inspire readers of all interests and abilities.

Index

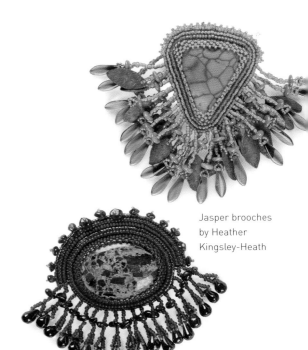

Jasper brooches
by Heather
Kingsley-Heath

Credits

Quarto would like to thank the following artists for kindly supplying jewellery for inclusion in this book.

- **Anita Seeberg** www.agronita.dk
- **Carol Mogg**
- **Christelle Greaves** www.handcraftedbyme.com
- **Colette Ladley** www.treasurecraft.co.uk
- **Diane Fairhall** dianefairhalldesigns@yahoo.co.uk
- **Gaile Almrott** www.breezy.biz
- **Heather Kingsley-Heath** www.heatherworks.co.uk
- **Heather Marrow** www.coordinatedimage.com
- **Jennifer Airs** www.jdjewellery.co.uk
- **Kanina Wolff** www.kanina.com
- **Karen Tan** www.lunarflares.com
- **Karin Chilton** www.sirius-jewellery.co.uk
- **Kim Booth** www.thepinkmartini.etsy.com
- **Kim Gover** www.bead-e-licious.co.uk
- **Lisa Taylor** www.bluetigerstudio.co.uk
- **Lorna Prime** www.pixiewillowdesigns.com
- **Maria Joao Rebelo** www.cooltemptations.com
- **Nan Fry** www.treasurecraft.co.uk
- **Peter Hoffman**
- **Philippa Wilson** paw750@btinternet.com
- **Sherril Olive** www.oliveoriginals.co.uk
- **Terry McCarthy**
- **Terry West** www.oceansdreamingdesigns.com
- **Trudi Doherty** www.glitteringprize.co.uk
- **Vicki Honeywill** www.pureshorelampwork.co.uk

Quarto would also like to thank Shutterstock for the images on pages 12, 13, 15, 16–17, 42–43, and 112–113.

All other images are the copyright of Quarto Publishing plc. While every effort has been made to credit contributors, Quarto would like to apologize should there have been any omissions or errors, and would be pleased to make the appropriate correction for future editions of the book.

Author's acknowledgments

I'd like to thank my family for all their support, patience and encouragement, and to dedicate this book to my mum, and to my dad who, although he is no longer with us, I think would be proud of my work.

I'd also like to thank all the contributors for providing such wonderful material, everyone at Quarto for making this writing experience such a positive one and for being so easy to work with, and thanks also go to all the girls at *The End of the Rainbow* for their continued support.